"Sisters were the foot soldiers of Catholic education. Those of us who marched with them are glad we did. *Don't Chew Jesus!* gives us a chance to relive that journey."

JOHN POWERS
Author of *Do Patent Leather Shoes Really Reflect Up?*

"My earliest memories from kindergarten and all the way through high school were of the Sisters of the Immaculate Heart of Mary (IHM) from Scranton. I only had one class in all of those years that was not taught by an IHM nun. I have to say that it was the poorest class I had in all of those years since all of the nuns were superb, from kindergarten through high-school graduation. Like so many other students of that time, I am forever in their debt and keep them in my prayers daily for a happy eternity following their wonderful lives on earth."

REV. THEODORE M. HESBURGH, C.S.C.
President Emeritus
University of Notre Dame

Don't Chew Jesus!

A Collection of Memorable Nun Stories

DANIELLE SCHAAF & MICHAEL PRENDERGAST

BenBella Books, Inc.
Dallas, Texas

BenBella Books, Inc.
6440 N. Central Expressway, Suite 617
Dallas, TX 75206
www.benbellabooks.com
Send feedback to feedback@benbellabooks.com

Printed in the United States of America
10 9 8 7 6 5 4 3 2

Library of Congress Cataloging-in-Publication Data

Schaaf, Danielle.
    Don't chew Jesus! : a collection of memorable nun stories / Danielle Schaaf and Michael Prendergast.
        p. cm.
    Includes bibliographical references (p.).
    ISBN 1-932100-82-2
    1.Nuns—Anecdotes. 2.Catholic schools—Anecdotes.I. Prendergast, Michael. II. Title.
    BX4205.S33 2006
    271'.903073--dc22

                                                                2006021674

Proofreading by Stacia Seaman and Jennifer Thomason
Cover design by Laura Watkins
Text design and composition by John Reinhardt Book Design
Printed by Bang Printing

Distributed by Independent Publishers Group
To order call (800) 888-4741
www.ipgbook.com

For special sales contact Yara Abuata at yara@benbellabooks.com

To my dearest "Publics"—my husband Mark
and children Catherine, Andrew, and Alex
D. S.

To my loving wife, Mary Lou,
a fellow Catholic-school survivor
M. P.

Acknowledgments

THANKS TO ALL OF YOU WHO shared your memories. Some of you brave souls are identified in this book; many requested anonymity. Still, others are anonymous because we lost contact: e-mails bounced, phones were disconnected, correspondence returned undeliverable, our tape recorder broke down, we couldn't read our own handwriting (both of us were Palmer Method failures, much to Sister B's chagrin), and our aging memories failed. *Mea Culpa.*

We are deeply grateful to the nuns themselves. We changed their names to protect their identities, along with those of us not so innocent. Many of the women remembered in the book have passed on. Sadly, a large number of the surviving sisters are retired with little financial support. In that end, we applaud the good works of the nonprofit group S.O.A.R.! (Support Our Aging Religious) and are donating a portion of our proceeds to them.

Special acknowledgment to our sweet "flowers"—Rosemary and Rose, a former nun and novice who guided us into the inner workings of day-to-day nun life. We also thank the wonderful folks at BenBella Books: Glenn Yeffeth, Publisher; Jennifer Thomason, Editor; Laura Watkins, Vice-President of Marketing; and Yara Abuata, Production Manager. We treasure your enthusiasm and support for this book. Thanks to Eileen Petrancosta for supplying photos of her and Sr.

Mary Louisette, BVM and Sr. Mary Theota, SSND. Recognition goes to Carrie, Colleen, Elizabeth, Jill, Karen, Kris, Maggie, Marina, Maureen, Sara, and Yvonne—members in a creative and multitalented writing group whose support was immeasurable.

Thanks to our spouses, children, families, and former classmates at St. Luke's. We especially thank our nuns, the Sisters of Mercy. Our memories of them take us back to simpler, black-and-white days of our youth and, in a humorous and sometimes roundabout way, to our faith in Christ and His Church.

Confession

Bless us, Father, for we have sinned.

Well, not exactly. But we haven't shared the whole story about *Don't Chew Jesus!* either. Yeah, we realize a sin of omission can bring us a stiff penance but we're hoping for full absolution with this confession. By now you've probably figured from the cover that *Don't Chew Jesus!* is a lighthearted, nostalgic book about Catholic nuns. After flipping through the first couple of pages, you'll find the book brimming with anecdotes guaranteed to take "readers of a certain age" hurtling back in time to a classroom patrolled by women in black (without the shades). But *Don't Chew Jesus!* is much more than a road trip home. Through hundreds of recollections and memories shared by contributors, *Don't Chew Jesus!* is a look back at a group of remarkable women and the impact they had on millions of us.

Writing this book was a journey that began more than forty years ago when we stepped through the doorways of St. Luke Catholic School. That's when we met our first nun—and each other. We spent the next eight years in a classroom together, usually sitting close enough to pass notes and whisper without getting caught. Well, most of the time we didn't get caught. We told each other jokes (usually irreverent), quizzed each other on the previous night's homework (which didn't last long since neither of us could read the other's handwriting), and chattered on about the nuns (usually not letting the sisters catch on to what we were doing). We didn't realize it at the time, but we were creating memories that would become the basis for *Don't Chew Jesus!*

We hung on to those memories when we moved on to public high school and then to the University of Florida. A quick passing on campus always came with a story and laugh about the sisters we no longer had as teachers. Decades later, after we went our separate ways and pursued careers, married spouses, and started families, a chance meeting on the street would turn into a stroll down memory lane with the nuns almost right by our side. *Don't Chew Jesus!* was taking shape.

Creating *Don't Chew Jesus!* began in earnest in a manner familiar to all those taught by nuns of yesteryear: a group of middle-age former Catholic-school students gathering over a few beers at a class reunion and gabbing about old times. Naturally, talk turned to nuns. Tossing back and forth stories like hand grenades ready to explode, we remembered it all—the good, the bad, and the ugly.

If an evening with friends and a few cold ones could open a floodgate of flashbacks, then we figured there might be a few more memory dams aching to burst. That was an understatement. We're still looking for that little Dutch boy to give us a hand. Just as whenever two or more Southerners get together and conversation turns to cockroaches, the gathering of a two or more taught by nuns sets lips yapping and anecdotes flying. We heard "I had this nun one time...." nearly as often as we had heard "you cheeky child, you!"

We systematically set out to collect stories by speaking before church groups, posting requests on Internet sites, and generating coverage in newspapers and radio. Nearly 400 stories rolled in, mostly from those, like us, who attended Catholic schools before 1970. Non-Catholics had their tales, too, as did several nuns and former nuns. Most were silly, innocuous anecdotes from days gone by but many were poignant memories that left a lump in our throats. Still, others were sad, sometimes scary, recollections that knotted our stomachs and had us sitting on the palms of our hands. Sisters were dedicated, passionate women who touched millions of us in ways we will never forget, and, in most cases, always appreciate. The stories flowed.

So here's the full confession: we started on this journey as a nostalgic lark. We thought we'd collect a few silly anecdotes that we could circulate in e-mails to other "Sister Survivors." Never did we envision the outpouring. Tales rolled in from all corners of the United States, and from England, Ireland, Canada, and Germany, as well. We were moved by how the idea of *Don't Chew Jesus!* moved our contributors. One gentleman stopped midway through his story to choke down tears. Another contributor tried telling his story to the telephone message recorder but gave up because he couldn't stop laughing.

We are stunned by the emotional chord *Don't Chew Jesus!* has struck. We didn't realize the void sisters left behind until hearing the recollections of so many others. You see, it hadn't fully dawned on us the nuns we knew truly were gone. Many are deceased and others are living in retirement. There are fewer nuns today replacing the older sisters and those who do, for the most part, are serving in areas outside the classroom. We were among the last wave to be taught by nuns. Indeed, we may be "The Greatest Generation" of Catholic schoolchildren.

For us, *Don't Chew Jesus!* has become more than a blast to the past. It's a link to our heritage, a legacy we can share with our children and grandchildren. To this end, perhaps *Don't Chew Jesus!* can help preserve the dedication, passion, and influence of these women. At the very least, we hope our readers will feel the same way.

Contents

Prologue

1965

Sister Clement faced the class, her brow crinkled and lips pursed. Absentmindedly, the tiny nun fingered the rosary beads hanging from her waist. Devout Catholic Boy wiggled in his seat while Devout Catholic Girl sat as still as holy water. Sister had been preparing the children to receive their First Holy Communion.

"Whaddya think is up with her," Devout Catholic Boy whispered as he fidgeted with a pencil on his desk.

"Shush," said Devout Catholic Girl, never taking her eyes off the nun pacing back and forth in front of them.

"Children, heed these words," Sr. Clement said. "The communion host contains the true body and blood of Jesus Christ. You must treat Him with honor and respect."

"Don't chew Jesus!"

"Just suck on Him."

"Whazzat? Did she say what I thought she said?" Devout Catholic Boy asked as nervous titters swept the classroom. Devout Catholic Girl closed her eyes and made the sign of the cross.

"Never let your teeth touch Jesus' body," Sister Clement continued. She finished her Catechism lesson with a smacking, tongue-thrusting demonstration. Placing an unblessed wafer on her tongue, Sr. Clement told the children:

"Puth Thethuth to the woof of yor mouf and thlet Him thitholve."

Devout Catholic Boy and Girl learned an important lesson that morning. Nuns would take whatever measures necessary to make certain their students grew into morally responsible adults. The children realized embarrassment, lack of facts, unruly students, or worldly influences would not stand in a nun's way. Sisters were women on a mission.

When we were kids, nuns were everywhere. Schools, playgrounds, churches, in our minds...they were always with us. We never thought about them not being around but that's exactly what happened. Somehow, they slipped away without our noticing. All that's left are memories and those of us who share those memories. Every time we'd bump into each other—in the halls at high school, at a University of Florida football game, or at one of our class reunions—we'd share stories about the nuns.

We aren't the only ones, either. Get two or more of us "older" Catholics together and conversation invariably turns to the nuns. Thoughts become one, each finishing the other's tale because experiences were the same, no matter where we lived or what order of sisters taught us. We marvel at the memories and briefly wonder what ever happened to the sisters. Then we move on to another story, and another, until it's time to say goodbye. That is, until the next time we bump into a fellow "Sister Survivor" and swap more stories.

M. P. and D. S.

Chapter One

Oh Sister, Where Art Thou?

"WHAT'S A NUN?"

"Don't be a smart-aleck, Yvonne," Mrs. Ogle told her fourth graders. That morning's CCE instructions called for discussing vocations such as joining the priesthood or becoming a nun. "You know, women who join religious orders and spend their lives totally devoted to God."

None of her students responded.

"Women who take vows of poverty, chastity, obedience?"

Nothing. Not a word from the nine-year-olds, most too young to know the meaning of chastity and none of them keen on poverty or obedience.

"They're called 'sisters' and wear special clothing that sometimes includes a veil?"

Finally, a hand in the back of the room crept upward.

"Yes, Maggie."

"My parents told me about sisters from the olden days. They were really old, even older than you, Mrs. Ogle," Maggie explained as her classmates snickered. "And they didn't have hair!"

"Um, Maggie, that's not exactly true."

"Some were really fun. My mother remembers playing hopscotch with them," Maggie went on. "And they were smart, too. Dad says they seemed to always know what he was up to, even before he knew. Sorta like mom, I guess."

"Mrs. Ogle, tell us more about sisters! Where are they now?" her class pleaded.

Nuns had been fixtures in Catholic schoolrooms for decades. As permanent as Latin Mass and meatless Fridays, sisters were a part of every Catholic kid's routine—like it or not.

From the time they awoke until after nightly prayers, Catholic schoolchildren's lives were touched by nuns. Mark would run straight past his bowl of Puffa Puffa Rice and into the bathroom every morning so he could dig night gunk out of his ears. He figured Sister Anastasia would be inspecting them later that day. Kris would scoot out the door and grab her uniform beanie knowing Sister Elizabeth would be standing at the church doorway checking for head coverings. How Kris hated getting stuck with a makeshift veil, one of Sr. Elizabeth's old tissues that she pulled out of her oversized sleeves like a magic trick and bobby-pinned not-so-gently on barren heads.

Outside Catholic schools, nuns' austere habits and sheltered lifestyles veiled them from most of the world. They were novelties, even to cradle Catholics. To casual observers, they were God's angels, creatures of mystery cloaked in awe. To millions of Catholics, nuns were teachers, nurses, confidantes, spiritual mothers, and defenders of the faith. Living symbols of piety, hope, and charity, they were simply "sisters." And they were everywhere.

Like military recruits answering a call to duty, hundreds of thousands of women enlisted in God's army as foot soldiers serving in America. Hometown girls, often inspired by sisters who taught them, signed up by the dozens. Some even went on to establish their own orders. Sister Elizabeth Seton formed the Sisters of Charity, while Mother Katharine Drexel founded the Sisters of the Blessed Sacrament for Indians and Colored People during the nineteenth century. Both eventually became saints.

Others traveled from afar, participants in a spiritual French Foreign Legion fulfilling a sacred mandate. For example, Sisters of Mercy came from God's country, Ireland, to spread His holy word and the legend of St. Patrick but not necessarily in that order. The nuns established missions in America that brought them face-to-face with war, disease, and anti-Catholic hatred. By the 1950s, nuns' front lines shifted to baby-boomer classrooms. Sisters took on new battles—shielding youngsters from Elvis's pelvis and Marilyn's pucker. This proved a more daunting battle than war, disease, and anti-Catholic hatred.

While nuns came from and taught in different places, the experiences they bestowed on their charges were eerily the same. Whether preparing youngsters to receive the Church's sacraments or explaining to them what little *they* knew about the facts of life, nuns everywhere seemed to teach from the same handbook.

Children who had never met and lived thousands of miles apart from each other in Brooklyn and Los Angeles learned blood oozed out of the communion host if they bit into it. They were chewing Jesus, sisters explained. Students in Pittsburgh and Buffalo reported the price for chewing gum in their schools was having it stuck to their noses. Almost universally, adolescent girls were taught to be wary of boys wearing patent leather shoes. After all, they *did* reflect up!

Occasionally, inquisitive (and nervy) children asked sisters how their lessons could be the gospel truth when their sources couldn't be tracked down. Searches of the Gospels, *Baltimore Catechism*, and even *Mad Magazine* revealed no such information, youngsters claimed. Good nuns everywhere referred to their manuals and delivered identical responses: "It's a divine mystery."

Whether on target or not, sisters delivered the Church's teachings, along with an outstanding secular education, with passion and verve. They did so using their own recipe: mixing large doses of determination and motivation with a pinch of fear and throwing in a touch of palm swatting to taste.

By 1965, a record 5.5 million children attended Catholic schools staffed almost entirely by nuns. Parents deposited their children on sisters' doorsteps each Monday morning, just as their parents and grandparents had done. Stepping into a class taught by nuns was just one more Catholic ritual, like toting tuna sandwiches to school each

Friday or lining up for weekly confession on Saturdays. Children blossomed under the sisters' unwavering devotion while the nuns' firm discipline helped students settle into the required one-size-fits-all learning environment. Sisters taught students both to love and fear God. Along the way, children grew to love and fear the nuns, too.

"*What was in the beginning, is now, and forever shall be.*" Every Catholic embraced the notion that life with nuns would be everlasting.

That was not to be.

Nearly overnight and much like the habits they wore, nuns seemed to disappear. Perhaps the ninety-hour workweek wore them down, or maybe it was facing fifty or sixty students at a time, but it looked as if God's army went AWOL.

Many weren't physically gone, but their identifiable marks were. Missing were head-to-toe shrouds, monastic lifestyles, and traveling in packs like wolves. Sisters traded in their medieval drapes for street-length attire but kept their trademark black shoes. They replaced flowing, offbeat headdresses with petite veils exposing *hair* for the first time. Names changed, too. Mystic-sounding Sr. Euphrasia became Sr. Sara while masculine Mother Paul turned into Sr. Karen.

Oh, Sister, where art thou? Why hast thou left?

The Catholic Church's Second Vatican Ecumenical Council—Vatican II—which convened in 1962, set forth a wave of modernization and unleashed the "Church's revolution," as one man described it. Trying to open up to the masses, the Church gave itself an overhaul that created more angst than the switchover from *Bewitched*'s Darrin #1 to Darrin #2.

Face-to-face reconciliation replaced anonymous dark-room confessions, and priests no longer had their backs to congregations during Mass. Along with the facelift came serious house cleaning, discarding centuries-old practices to a holy landfill. Latin Mass, mandatory head coverings for women, and nuns themselves, it seemed, were tossed aside like St. Christopher's relics. Worst of all to some, silent head nodding replaced moaning breast thumping, and parishioners actually *touched* each other with handshakes during Mass. Some married couples even kissed, in church, for Godless sake! What were elderly churchwomen to make of it all?

When Vatican II Council ended in 1965, nearly 180,000 sisters served in the United States. The next year, that number began to decline; by 2004, the Church counted fewer than 75,000 nuns in its service. Sisters were disappearing. Some searched out new front lines serving the poor and less fortunate. Others simply left their orders. Compounding the matter, new recruits weren't joining in large enough numbers to replace departures. Sisters had all but vanished, relegating a significant chunk of Catholic heritage to memories. What memories those were!

Nuns were much more than stereotypical knuckle-crackers and pious disciples. Filled with a bulldog's determination and the single-minded passion of a hungry farm cat stalking its prey, sisters created uniquely colorful experiences for generations of schoolchildren. From those adventures came inspired storytelling.

Driven by a poker player's up-the-ante mentality, yarn spinners tried outdoing each other. Nun-story-swapping evolved into a form of entertainment, typically beginning when a couple of students gathered together outside parish grounds "Sister Gerald caught me talking in the bathroom line and made me clean out the stalls for a week," one youngster might begin, quickly folding when his companion topped him with a tale of Sr. Mary Cavanaugh chasing down a student through the parking lot after he told her homework was a "crappy idea."

From there, storytelling one-upmanship evolved into a vocation to "Go forth and share the truth." Some of the most powerful tales came out of religious beliefs and practices that sisters taught their students.

Stephanie (Sellers) Mazzon recalled her First Holy Communion fiasco in Seymour, Indiana. She lived out every second grader's communion nightmare—vomiting. She threw up Jesus! More than thirty years later, she cringed at the memory while her listener blanched, remembering her own Sister Mary Joseph's admonition never to touch Jesus' body—let alone spew Him out.

Sisterly discipline triggered some of the most captivating memories. One woman talked about the day a nun banished her to a closet. After Sr. Georgiana caught Betsy Adams crowing like a rooster to her classmates, she decided the teenager needed more time practicing her newly found talent. Sister forced Adams to spend an hour in a cloakroom crowing the entire time.

Another man recalled a classmate presenting a bamboo stick to a sister as a gift. Maybe the young boy hoped she would thank him for his gesture by "sparing the rod" the next time he got out of line. No such luck. Like the mad scientists on so many cartoon shows of the day, the boy was doomed by his own invention and earned the privilege of allowing Sister to break in the gift on him.

Poignant memories demonstrating nuns' powerful influence have made for stirring storytelling. An elderly woman tearfully recalled the day more than fifty years earlier when doctors advised her and her husband not to have any additional children. Their firstborn child was diagnosed with cystic fibrosis, a genetic, fatal disease. Distraught, the couple confided in Sr. Cecelia. Sister Cecelia was more than a spiritual advisor to the couple; she was the woman's blood-sister.

"Don't fret," Sister Cecelia told the couple. "Remember, God will give you no more than you can bear." Her unflinching faith convinced the couple to have more children. They produced eight more children, none suffering from the deadly disease.

Many stories moved beyond nostalgic recollections to legends-in-the-making. Tales of gate-hurdling nuns, nuns toting guns, and even bare-all skinny-dipping sisters surfaced, opening the doors for new material to entertain future audiences.

Although old-style Catholic nuns have slipped away, memories shared by the millions they touched will never fade. Recollections become more meaningful each time they're passed along, as New Yorker Tamara Valles revealed with her remembrances of a special sister:

Sister Bon Bon Lives On
As a reporter for the *Staten Island Advance*, part of my job has been reviewing the paper as it came off the presses, checking for mistakes.

Sometimes I was fortunate to have the time to peruse the paper from a reader's perspective. One Monday, enjoying just that luxury, I flipped through the pages and paused to read a few stories.

I stopped at the obituary page. As a twenty-five-year-old, I didn't often read that page unless I was reviewing an obituary I had written. For some reason, maybe because it was a slow news day or I just had a few extra minutes, I skimmed the listings. A name jumped off the page:

"Sister Bonaventure Scarangella"

My mind spun backward to when I was a small child. My parents and grandparents often told me many stories about the nuns who taught them. The tales that stuck out most in my mind were those about how the naughty children were disciplined—hands mercilessly slapped with rulers, girls' hair and boys' ears pulled, and kids forced to stand in a classroom corner for hours. Although those stories frightened me, I didn't dwell on them. I attended public school, after all.

I began to worry about those stories when, as an eleven-year-old, I was enrolled in Catholic school. Trying to calm myself, I reasoned that nuns were devoted to God and probably much sweeter, kinder, gentler folks than those remembered by older family members. They were admirable women bearing qualities of honesty, love, and respect, right?

On their good days, they were. On their not-so-good days...well, God help the soul who crossed them. Especially if the nun happened to be Sr. Bonaventure.

Sister "Bon Bon" gave new meaning to the word "tough." She was born and raised in Brooklyn, possessing that city's trademark attitude and accent. If anyone broke the rules, Sister Bon Bon could be counted on to share a few very *loud* words with the culprit. Subtlety, thy name was not Sister Bon Bon.

Sister usually backed up her words with action, sometimes in creative ways. Caught chewing gum in class? Bon Bon stuck it on your nose, where it stayed for the day. Didn't turn in your spelling homework? Sister required you to write the words hundreds of times or until your wrist turned limp. Dared to clown around, interrupt the class, and generally act like a bratty kid? Bon Bon forced offenders to kneel by their desks for an hour or so, never allowing them to lean back on their heels.

I was one of the overachievers in Sister's class and usually didn't rile her merciless side. However, I never did take the hint that I talked too much in her class! She scolded me about that more times than I care to remember.

It was easy to whine about Sister's stern demeanor and to protest that we could never get away with anything. She seemed to have eyes in the back of her habit! When we weren't fussing over Sister's rigid manner, we moaned about her drill-sergeant techniques, such as requiring us to repeat over and over again in a sing-song fashion a list of one hundred prepositions or the eight parts of speech.

Sister also freely dished out advice, sometimes even evoking a chuckle or two from us. Whenever the classroom topic turned to sex and dating, which happened quite often during my inquisitive pre-teen years, Sr. Bon Bon admonished us with: "Remember, girls, no one will want to buy the cow if the milk is given away for free."

As rough as Sister Bon Bon seemed, I now realize she was trying to prepare me for life. Her job was to produce first-class students with the intentions of turning them into well-educated, decent, moral adults. She took to that vocation with passion and drive.

As I read Sister's obituary, I was taken aback with shock and genuine sadness. Remorse hit me hard, too, as I regretted not visiting her after my eighth-grade graduation and for never making the time to write her a letter, thanking her for everything she meant to me. And now she was gone.

I was struck by a parting thought as I lay down the obituaries and turned to my job as a features writer. I hoped my subjects and verbs always agreed and that I used my prepositional phrases in precisely the right way. Sister Bonaventure, perched above in heaven, would easily discover otherwise and certainly find a way to make me repent my grammatical sins. Rightly so, too.

God bless you, Sr. Bon Bon. Rest in peace.

My years with the nuns were filled with learning prayers, memorizing the *Baltimore Catechism*, preparing for and learning how not to "chew Jesus." But nothing is more memorable than when Sister put the fear of God in me. Actually, it was a fear of hell.

For hell to have meaning, Sister first taught us how perfect heaven was. It was a place where you'd find candy, your favorite food, no homework, or your dead hamster from kindergarten brought back to life. Generally, heaven was pretty much the opposite of what I was going through in second grade.

Hell was another matter. Words alone couldn't adequately convey the despair of an eternity roasting in an all-consuming fire, so Sister relied on St. John's Catechism Film Strip series. Even though there was no color and sound was iffy, the movie presented a horrific depiction of hell complete with fire, brimstone, and revolting characters.

It showed new arrivals to hell: a blue-collar laborer, a perky housewife sporting a Jackie Kennedy pillbox hat, and a business executive wearing his gray power suit, skinny tie, and still toting a briefcase. None were too happy about walking through the inside of a giant Weber grill as the devil and his creepy companions leered and poked at them. The only thing missing was Jason in his hockey mask.

Despite my fear, I was able to understand Sister's teachings that God was loving and forgiving. Watching that film was enough for me to think, "Surely, heaven and God must be the opposite of this."

M. P.

Chapter Two

Don't Chew Jesus!

S ISTER MARY PATRICK STEPPED OUTSIDE the convent, blessed herself in the sign of the cross, and charged up the walkway on a mission. Her job: assure the delivery of fifty young souls into heaven.

Catholic religious education was a nun's number-one priority. Sure, praying for lost souls in purgatory or helping Father call out bingo numbers played a big role in her life, but dispensing the "One True Word" was most nuns' calling. Sister Mary Patricks in parishes from Missoula, Montana to Lafayette, Louisiana, had nearly identical lessons in store for Catholic children, instructing them in the same tenets, prayers, and rituals.

Parents pitched in, too, teaching morning prayers, before-meal blessings, and making sure kids showed up to weekly confession. Hard-core beliefs and practices, however, were left to the professionals. Sister Mary Patrick's lesson plan might have included these Catholic basics along with personalized notations:

Monday: Drill children on Chapter 1, *Baltimore Catechism*, 6Q: Why did God make you? *Don't let Carrie suck you into questions like why did God make communists, Lex Luthor, and other evil people.*

Tuesday: Emphasize the importance of being Catholic. Remind students only Catholics are allowed in heaven and offer prayers for neighborhood Protestants. (*Be sure to think of our grocer, Mr. Morrow. Maybe he'll remember to add fish to his meat case on Fridays.*)

Wednesday: Tour the church and show children the two-finger holy water dip. Demonstrate genuflecting without holding on to the pew.

Thursday: Practice May Crowning procession. Line up students shortest to tallest. (*Need to reorder the line. Colleen's gone through a growth spurt and she's taller than Chuck.*)

Friday: Review saint of the week, St. Amaburga, patron saint for prevention of bruises. (*Children have been a bit rough on the playground.*)

Nuns who taught children Catholic doctrine trudged along a path laden with obstacles. With the pluck of St. Pantaleon, a martyr who survived six torturous attempts on his life, sisters molded youths into model children of God by relying on creativity and passion. Nuns pulled out all stops, using inventive storytelling, embellishment, poetic license, and catechism films demonstrating the horrors of hell to illustrate complex points.

One of the toughest lessons involved explaining transubstantiation—the belief that through the power of God, priests could bless thin wafers of bread during Mass and transform them into an edible vessel holding Jesus' body. Educating adults on how Jesus' body and blood could be contained in the communion host had always been a daunting task for theologians, but for a nun facing a room full of second graders? As easy as nabbing a spitballer before the wad left his mouth.

Students were warned by heaven's earthly gatekeepers that they must never touch Jesus with their hands, much less inflict pain on him with their teeth. Nuns unleashed a "Don't Chew Jesus" rally cry, and with it horrific tales of anguish, pain, and blood-spilling if they did.

"We had solid proof that Jesus' body was in the host," Kathy Cramer recalled. "The nuns talked about an incident where a young girl spat out the communion host into her handkerchief. The hankie turned to blood, they said!"

Even worse than chewing Jesus was spewing Him. Students recall learning to avoid the lavatory (nuns never called them bathrooms, much less "johns") if they felt a holy hurl coming on. Jesus wasn't to be flushed away like the pet alligator your aunt brought home from Florida but deposited in a receptacle (nunspeak for "bowl"). Then, Father would bury the bowl like the statue of St. Joseph many Catholics planted in their gardens to help sell their houses.

Teaching children to "make a good confession" was another potential stumbling block sisters faced. By the age of seven, youngsters automatically had crossed an imaginary line into the world of sin but many had difficulty knowing exactly where the boundary lay. Sisters offered reminders to the children that they were now capable of committing mortal sin by, for example, eating a bologna sandwich on Friday. Still, children remained uncertain of what was a sin and what wasn't.

Sister-is-it-a-sin-if questions bounced around second-grade classrooms faster than hurling balls in a Jai Alai arena. Most questions were asked in the third person, presumably to help out a potential lost soul but in reality protecting one's own identity. A typical rambling question might have been asked like this: "I have this friend, Sister, who really wanted to go to Mass on Sunday but who kind of had to miss it because her Protestant friends were going to the beach and asked her to come and it would have hurt their feelings if she said no. Was that a sin?"

Nuns realized this uncertainty could lead millions of blackened souls directly to hell, or at least to a bazillion years in purgatory. Under that kind of pressure sisters weren't above intimidating young children into examining their consciences and spilling the beans. Besides, what better opportunity to put the fear of God into children than during confession?

Children were taught their path to heaven began behind the confessional door, in a room no bigger than a closet and as pitch black as their souls. Most loathed stepping into that room where the sole illumination peeked through pinholes in a screen separating them from the priest. Loathing turned to fear as young confessors mentally ticked off sins while waiting for slate-cleaning time to begin when

Father slid open the screen door. To calm children, sisters explained their sins were safe with Father; he would never reveal them. Not even a Communist's threat of torture or a mom's bribe of homemade chocolate cake would cause him to tell all. Both tactics probably had been tried in the past and failed miserably.

More fearsome than revealing sins in the confessional, however, was not telling them at all. And nuns knew that, too.

"For weeks leading up to our First Confession, Sr. Bruno constantly reminded us to confess all our sins so we would be able to receive our First Communion in a pure state," recalled Marina Schmidt. "I was only in second grade and didn't have very many sins.

"I made some up so I would at least sound like a sinner."

Schmidt's First Confession went on without a hitch and the following morning she joined her classmates for one final pep talk from Sr. Bruno before receiving communion for the first time.

"Worms will wiggle right out of your mouth if you stick out your tongue to receive communion and there is still a sin on your soul," Sr. Bruno said. "That will be Father's sign to refuse you communion."

Schmidt realized her confession was full of lies. Lying to a priest! Panicked, she struck a deal with God.

"First I prayed for no worms. Then I prayed for tiny worms that no one could see." Schmidt reported no worms that day, just the creation of a lifelong memory of Sr. Bruno.

Nuns relied on more than fear to impart the faith to young ones. First and foremost, their own dedication to God served as examples. Penny Reed remembered the time Sr. Philomena called her into an empty classroom and asked her to kneel with her in front of a trash can. Wise enough to not disobey a nun, Reed knelt beside Sr. Philomena.

"Do you see Him?"

"Who, Sister?"

"Him, Him! Jesus!" the nun shouted, pointing to the trash can.

Jesus emblazoned the outside of the trash can. At least Sister thought so. Reed admitted she didn't see anything but continued meeting with the nun each day in a lunchtime prayer to trash-can Jesus.

"Just because I couldn't see Him doesn't mean Sr. Philomena couldn't. I figured the holiest of people probably could see Jesus in things like trash cans."

Just like Whoopi Goldberg in *Sister Act*, many nuns were blessed with sharp wit. Delivering doctrine with a dose of humor helped offset the fear of God they placed in children.

At St. Agnes Academy, Sr. Mary Regina asked Michelle Pennington and her classmates what they thought the initials *INRI* nailed to the top of Jesus' cross meant. No one answered.

"Well, it sure doesn't stand for I'm Nailed Right In," the nun said, prompting Pennington and her friends to burst into a fit of giggles.

When fear and humor weren't enough to get across a religious concept, nuns fell back on a fail-safe Catholic technique: guilt. Masters of spiritual blackmail, nuns could out-guilt a roomful of Jewish mothers. Mary (Behrens) Gerardi recalls learning that for every blank piece of paper she threw into the trash, she would earn ten days in purgatory.

Houstonian Kim Fazzino recalls a similar threat, but one that created even more remorse. "For every wad of paper we threw at the garbage can and missed, we delayed *someone else's* soul from getting out of purgatory, sisters told us."

Catholic schoolchildren lived in a state of continual stress knowing they could become purgatory's trash collectors.

Everyone knew Sister had the final say, even if it didn't mesh with official dogma. This was especially apparent when explaining who got into heaven—and who didn't. Catholics hit by cars as they crossed a street on their way to confession weren't the only poor souls not passing through heaven's gates. For non-Catholics, the pearlies were chained and locked, according to a few nuns. These teachings weren't found in catechism books but, since Sister said so, it must be true. To schoolchildren, Sister's word was as infallible as the pope's.

"Sisters told us that to get into heaven we must all be Catholic," recalled Laurie (Keenan) Sheldon, who attended St. James Catholic School in Kearney, Nebraska. "I passed the public school on my walk home each day and I could hear the kids and their teachers going about daily lessons.

"Just thinking of all my non-Catholic friends not being allowed into such a wonderful place such as heaven created a stressful burden," she said.

"That seemed much too difficult for a small child like me to bear."

Always purveyors of hope, nuns offered a way non-Catholics could enter heaven—convert to Catholicism. In fact, one nun in Wisconsin offered a two-for-one incentive. According to Corinne Dorey, the nun told Dorey's grandmother that Catholics gained automatic admission for themselves if they helped a non-Catholic join the faith.

"Nana smothered my son Nick with hugs, kisses, and *Glory Be's* when she discovered he not only directed a classmate to the Church but also the young boy's parents," Dorey said, adding she regarded her grandmother's reactions as a little "over the top."

The elderly woman explained to Dorey that years ago when she attended St. Wenceslaus, nuns promised admission into heaven for those who shepherded converts to the Catholic faith.

"If the nuns said it, and my grandmother believed it, it must be true," Dorey said.

Nuns drilled home lessons with hefty doses of physical interaction. First Communion preparation included practicing sucking, not chewing, Jesus-less hosts. Training for confession meant Sister role-played the priest while kids out-sinned each other with made-up offenses like stealing money out of the poor box or murdering their teachers.

Nuns realized rituals and routines helped children see, hear, and feel the full effect of their religious education. Pageants and processions gave sisters the best opportunities to involve all the senses. Walking in a May Crowning procession, children fingered their rosary beads while chanting familiar prayers and singing rounds of "Bring Flowers of the Rarest." During Lent, sisters led children on Jesus' last walk, reenacting His last moments at each of fourteen Stations of the Cross.

RELIGIOUS HABITS

Sister says:

1. During prayer, hold hands upright with palms facing each other, fingers straight up just under the chin. Overlap thumbs, always right over left. Never, ever clasp hands, and God help anyone who drops his hands to his waist. *Kids cried every year after the First Holy Communion group photographs came out. It gave Sister another chance to go after hand-slackers she might have missed that day.*

2. Every time Jesus' name is said, it must be accompanied by a bow of the head. *This is why so many great Catholic baseball players like Yogi Berra and Joe Garagiola were catchers. Managers found it too risky to put them in the outfield where they might miss pop flies.*

3. When not using rosary beads, tuck them away in a reverent spot. Fabric pouches and plastic boxes are excellent choices but hanging them over a statue of the Virgin Mary is ideal. Never wear beads as jewelry, unless pretending to be a nun; and only then from the waistband. Hanging rosary beads from a rearview mirror is forbidden. Jesus deserves to be treated better than a pair of fuzzy dice.

4. When in church, always look forward, head held high. If the girl down the pew passes out, don't look. Kneel upright, never rest on your haunches. Don't ever think of parking your tush on the pew. *Dispensations were given to elderly women since they spent a lot of time on their knees in church praying for lost souls.*

While sisters were ushering millions of children along the path to heaven, their students wondered why they even bothered. What did it matter if a bunch of cheeky kids made it out of Catholic school, much less into heaven, some wondered.

One rumor floating up and down pews suggested the women were enrolled in a Catholic early release program. For every child landing safely in heaven, the celestial warden knocked a few days off a nun's stay in purgatory. Sister wasn't ticking off Hail Marys on her rosary beads but counting days to her pardon, some surmised.

That theory fell from grace as soon as speculators woke up and smelled the incense. Anyone watching Sr. Mary Patrick storm up the walkway each morning would have realized worrying about a layover in purgatory was the last thing on her or any other nun's mind. Surely, God had them booked on direct flights to heaven.

Religious Education Memories
The Basics: Don't Chew Jesus!

I'll Chew if I Want To

As she prepared us to receive Holy Communion for the first time, Sr. Mary Thomas preached over and over again that we would be receiving the body and blood of Christ. She warned us to not chew the wafer. Despite her repeated admonitions, Sr. Mary Thomas hadn't fully convinced me I would burn in hell if I chewed Jesus. Almost, but not quite.

When the day arrived, I joined my classmates at St. Michael's Church, an old-fashioned cathedral complete with stained glass, statues, and pillars. Dressed in a traditional virginal white dress and veil, I solemnly approached the altar where first I knelt and then I stuck out my tongue to receive communion.

I was determined to discover what would happen if I bit into the wafer. Instead of sucking and swallowing the host the way Sr. Mary Thomas taught us, I let it rest in my mouth until I returned to my pew. I took to heart some of what Sister said because before I bit down I tried to hide from her sight by kneeling behind one of the huge pillars. A fate worse than hell awaited me if she caught me with blood gushing out of my mouth.

I chewed the host. Nothing happened, at least not that day. Not long afterward my father died. For many years I thought I might have been partly responsible because I carried out the unthinkable that holy day.

But Why Can He Chew?

Returning to the classroom after daily Mass, Peter asked Sister why Father was allowed to chew Jesus and we weren't. Peter was referring to when the priest administers communion to himself and clearly chews the wafer.

As answers from nuns so often were, her response to this mystery of faith was a simple one. "His Jesus is bigger than yours, that's why."

The priest's communion host was a king-sized version of those we received so he could hold it aloft for everyone in the church to see.

Dirty, Grubby Hands

Sister Elizabeth taught us only priests' consecrated hands could touch the communion hosts because the wafers contained the body and blood of Jesus. As faithful Catholics, we learned early on that should we ever stumble upon free-ranging hosts, we should never touch them with our hands, out of respect for Jesus.

To illustrate the point, Sr. Elizabeth shared with us the story of a dutiful little boy who, on his walk home from school, spied a bunch of blessed wafers lying on the ground next to a chalice.

"This devoted boy, ever so mindful of his sinfully grubby hands, carefully picked up and returned Jesus' body to the chalice, host by host, using only his elbows," Sister explained.

Sister never explained *how* the little boy knew the hosts were consecrated, or how they disappeared from the church tabernacle where they were normally stored under lock and key. She also failed to explain how the boy's elbows managed to be holy enough to hold the hosts while his hands were not. That was her story and she was sticking to it.

Take-Home Jesus

The order of nuns who taught us, Ursulines, were responsible for making the hosts, or wafers, used in communion. When I was an altar boy, I would stuff my pockets with unblessed hosts and bring them home to snack on. My dad walked in on me one day and asked what I was eating.

"Communion hosts," I said, not giving it much thought.

Dad panicked. He ran out of the room, hollering, "Marina, come quick! Oh my God, Charlie's eating Jesus' body!"

"Oh my God, oh my God, what will we do?" Mom wailed. "A son of mine is eating the body of Christ!"

Mom called the parish priest who assured her the hosts were not consecrated and I was eating only bread. I got a licking anyway.

The Basics: The Catholic Way ... or Sister's?

Protestant Kneeling

I had a tendency to lean backward, resting on my calves, when I kneeled. I overheard one of the nuns say, "She even kneels like a Protestant."

Heaven's Not for Everyone

My younger sister came home from her first day of kindergarten upset, with tears streaming down her cheeks. It seems her teacher, Sister Ursula, told her that our parents would never go to heaven. Sister claimed they lost all chances for heavenly repose because my mother was a Protestant, and my dad married her—the second marriage for him! Apparently in the 1950s, these transgressions were enough to close the pearly gates on some people.

Thank God I'm a Catholic

Several times during the day the nuns instructed us to get out of our desks, stand tall, and pray, "Thank you, God, for making me a Catholic." I'm not sure if this was a reminder for us or for them.

The Basics: Beliefs and Almost Beliefs

Sharing Jesus

When she wasn't disciplining us, Sister was busy dispensing her own brand of Catholic dogma. She advised if we were ever seated next to someone who didn't receive communion, we should slightly touch that person on the shoulder after we returned from communion. That way we could transfer Jesus' blessings to them.

Devil on My Shoulder
As a boarding student at a girls' academy, I was expected to attend daily Mass at 6 A.M. It was very difficult to avoid nodding off to sleep. Sister Gabriel gave me an incentive, though. She convinced me that should I fall asleep in church, the devil would perch on my head.

Don't Be an Infant, Er...Baby
I remember my first-grade teacher Sr. Augustine wearing a permanent scowl on her face and continually berating us with insults when we did not behave. Calling us "infants" was one of her most frequent affronts.

Christmas was nearing, so Sr. Augustine was teaching us about Christ's birth. The more she spoke of Jesus, the more I grew convinced He must have done something very bad.

Sister Augustine kept calling Him "infant" Jesus, just as she frequently called me and the rest of my classmates when we misbehaved.

You Pray What?
I remember sisters teaching us ejaculations—short prayers or utterances—when an ambulance drove by or when we passed a cemetery or funeral procession. The word certainly took on a different meaning in adulthood!

Praying Hands
Sister taught us to pray with our hands clasped together and fingers pointed straight up. That way, we could send our prayers directly to heaven.

Letters to God
Good penmanship was very important to nuns. You could have kidnapped the Lindbergh baby and that would have been okay as long as

the ransom note was written neatly, flush with the left-hand margin, and with all the upper and lower loops properly and proportionately placed. Life was difficult for my fellow left-handers and me.

One day, the whole class had to write letters to God that only He would read. The plan was that Sr. Joseph would burn the letters and the smoke would carry them up to God in heaven so he could read them. Unfortunately for me, the official censor—Sr. Joseph—read the letters ahead of time. She decided my handwriting was so messy that even God could not read it.

Sister made me spend my whole lunch period rewriting my letter and still, the rewrite was not acceptable. God never got to read my letter because Sister refused to burn it.

Call an Ambulance

The sisters told us to carry our rosary beads with us at all times. If we were in an accident, bystanders would know to call a priest because we possessed the holy beads. I could just imagine the scene:

"Hold on, Officer, don't call an ambulance! See those rosary beads?" says a worried bystander. "You know what that means."

"Right, call a priest. Then we can get an ambulance over here."

That was the truth according to Sister.

Saving Spaces

When I was a kindergartner, Sister told me I had a guardian angel following me around. She said to leave space in my desk so the angel could sit with me. To this day, I don't take up the whole seat when I sit in my chair. I guess I'm still saving a place for my guardian angel!

Trip to Heaven

Sister told us a sure way to get into heaven: if we saw someone just about to get hit by a car, we should throw ourselves in front of it. I can't imagine telling young children to do such a thing!

Limbo Babies

I remember our sisters teaching us about limbo, the near-heavenly home where babies who died before they could be baptized were sent. It was so sad to think of sweet infants not being allowed into heaven. In fact, I liked to imagine that the Virgin Mother stood at limbo's back door, sneaking the babies out and into heaven. I couldn't quite imagine her letting infants float around in limbo for eternity.

Line Up for Limbo

The sisters taught us limbo was just like heaven but you didn't get to see God. Considering the rest of us faced the possibility of hell, which, based on scenes from a religious filmstrip series, did not look like a nice place, I recall thinking I wished I had been given a choice. Had I had been asked before baptism, I would have settled for the no-risk limbo option.

J. M. J.

The sisters taught us to sign our papers JMJ, short for "Jesus, Mary, and Joseph." It tickled me to hear author Mary Higgins Clark mention in one of her audio books that she thought the signature was created for her specially. You see, the writer thought it stood for her and her two brothers: "Joseph, Mary, and John."

The Basics: Sacrament Preparation

Sister's Influence

Sister taught us we could not eat or drink anything before we received Holy Communion. She not only impressed that requirement upon me, but on my mother, too. My mother tied a hankie around the faucet in our bathroom Sunday mornings as a reminder to not drink water before church.

Hotline to God

Sisters displayed posters that depicted the confessional as a phone booth with a direct line to God. This was sort of like the red phone that would connect the president to the Kremlin if we hit the brink of nuclear war.

Confession Etiquette

Inside the confessional, we knelt on a wooden step that triggered a switch (high-tech for those days) that would illuminate a ruby red light above the door outside. Sister taught us this was our warning system. First, it warned us not to enter because someone was inside. Second, it warned us to back up and/or stick our fingers in our ears to avoid hearing other people's sins. Listening to other people's sins was a sin itself. It might even be a mortal sin depending on whether our hearing was accidental, what kind of sins were overheard, and how much fun the situation created for the person listening to the sins.

Chains of Confession

When preparing us for our first confession, Sr. Hedwig stressed the importance of "making a good confession." To assert this point, she shared with us the story of a little boy who knowingly left out a sin. According to Sr. Hedwig, as soon as the boy stepped out of the confessional flames shot out of his mouth and his feet were shackled in chains.

The day of our First Confession, each of us took our turn in the confessional. As soon as we stepped out, most of us immediately turned around and went back into the little dark room to confess again. We were terrified to omit a sin, even if by accident.

I guess Monsignor Holt, who was hearing confessions, stopped us all and demanded to know why we were treating the confessional like a revolving door. Once we told him, Monsignor assured us that forgetting a sin wouldn't turn us into demons.

Confession Penance

I remember practicing for my First Confession and Sister role-played the priest. Trying to do a good job, I told her all the big sins like lying to your parents, saying shut up, and not being nice to my brother and sisters. Then I got a little carried away and told her I bit the dog and pulled the cat's tail. Never again! For my penance, she made me say a whole rosary.

Practice Makes Perfect

We prepared to make our First Confession with practice sessions where Sister John the Evangelist pretended to be Father. I remembered to start with "Bless me, Father, for I have sinned" and then followed it with a few imaginary sins. Sister gave me an easy penance of praying two Our Fathers. All went smoothly until I tried to leave the confessional. I kept pulling on the door to open it but I should have pushed it outward instead. Terror struck when I heard the screen door opening behind me for the second time. I tried explaining but Sister John was not amused. She gave me another penance.

Religious Crutch

For our souls to be cleansed of sin, we needed to "make a good confession," Sister Henrietta drilled into us as we prepared to receive the sacrament for the first time. To help us put it in perspective, she told us about a crippled boy who hobbled on crutches into the confessional. Apparently, he did an excellent job of "making a good confession" because he walked out without his crutches. We should remember that boy's example, she explained.

The morning of my First Confession, I stepped into the confessional and knelt. Looking upward, I remembered the crippled boy's good confession. How could I not? Hanging over my head was a pair of children's crutches!

Are You Kneeling?

Two days before we were scheduled to make our First Confession, Sister had us practice with her in the confessional. I knelt down in front of a small screen and Sister sat on the other side of it. Sister could only see my body from the waist up. She thought I was standing on the kneeler.

"Eddie, please kneel down," she said.

"But, Sister, I *am* kneeling."

Sister came out of the confessional and pulled back the curtain to see what I was up to. Sure enough, I was kneeling. Sister laughed. She had forgotten that I was one of the tallest boys in the class.

Confirmation Cuff

Sister Andrew Paul told us that as part of the sacrament of confirmation ceremony, we would be slapped on the face by the bishop. The sacrament was an initiation into Catholic adulthood, so I guessed the slap was a symbol that we "could take it." Nevertheless, I was disturbed at the thought of a confirmation cuff.

I grew anxious waiting to face the bishop. He was a big man and I was a small girl. My imagination ran wild! I had visions of me splayed out on the floor in front of the altar after being belted by the bishop.

Imagine my surprise when the bishop brushed my face with a light tap of his palm. I barely felt his touch!

The Basics: Feast Days

St. Blaise and Clear Throats

I taught at a Catholic school in New Orleans for three years and since I wasn't Catholic, it was a learning experience. I happily embraced all the saint days but I received a memo about one that surely was a misprint. A special Mass was being held the following Friday for the "blessing of the throats." I had been at the school for some time and had seen many saint days, and even learned about May Crownings, but this one threw me!

I thought surely the memo was wrong so I asked the high-school principal, Sr. Jerome, about its accuracy. She explained it was the Feast of St. Blaise, which called for a very nice ritual to ward off colds and sore throats. It was February and the height of winter season, and since I was the one who had twenty-five sneezers facing me every morning, I asked if I could be blessed. Sister gave me an enthusiastic yes.

So there I was, with all my first graders, kneeling at the altar with the candles crossing my throat. Amazingly, there were no colds for me that winter!

Christ the King Procession

Each year St. Rita's hosted a procession in honor of Christ the King feast day on the Saturday before the start of Advent season. The idea was for us to give glory to Jesus and to ask for reparation for sins, which we proclaimed publicly by walking the streets and singing hymns and waving palms. We finished by returning to the church for a traditional Latin Mass.

Sister Lucille produced the extravaganza and demanded a command performance by all 200 kids from St. Rita's. Attendance was mandatory. Not even children whose parents refused to bring them were excused.

Unfortunately, I was one of those unlucky few whose parents said no to the Saturday shuttle.

The following Monday, Sr. Lucille pulled out of class all students who didn't appear Saturday. She lined us up, pinning our backs against the wall. One by one, Sister slapped our cheeks and handed each of us a tiny straw symbolizing a stunted palm. Forming our own procession, we delinquents marched from classroom to classroom waving our pitiful straw sprigs and confessing to our peers how we skipped the real procession.

I realized Sr. Lucille's spectacle was an effort to belittle us. I didn't buy into it, nor did it affect me. Chalk it up to bizarre behavior, I thought. Evidently it was not the last of her peculiar oddities, as she ended her years institutionalized.

Just like public-school teachers, our sisters taught us all the basics: math, reading, English, science, and social studies. But since nuns didn't go home to families the way public-school teachers did, we figured they spent their spare time coming up with ways to, um, *enrich* our education.

While public-school kids spent afternoons riding bikes, we pored over tons of homework. The only exception was raising funds selling World's Finest Chocolates. "Publics" didn't have to worry about financing all that extra schoolwork.

"Publics" performed one-hour assemblies in the cafeteria. Our nuns booked an auditorium so we'd have curtains, lighting, and good acoustics for a show that had parents sneaking out after four hours. "Publics" took field trips to the zoo. We got a trip to the police station where we toured jail cells, learned booking procedures, and snatched our first look at a dead body—from photos spread over a detective's desk.

Nuns constantly threatened to ship us off to public school. We jumped at the idea of no homework but our parents wouldn't hear of it.

M. P. and D. S.

Chapter Three

*Off to School
with Publics You'll Go*

ISTER BAPTISTA STOOD CROSS-ARMED in the doorway, her face flushed and pinched like a lobster claw. She held her ground.

"Mikey O'Doul, I've warned you before, off you go."

Mikey drifted down the path to the street. Turning back for one last look, the second grader waved good-bye to his classmates lining the walkway. Resigned to his fate, Mikey took the last steps of a pariah; a death row inmate inching his way toward the chamber. Sr. Baptista had exiled Mikey to eternal wastelands—the local public school.

Mikey woke up, his Will Robinson jammies sodden with sweat. That dream again! "I'd better turn in my homework on time tomorrow," he thought as he buried his head into the pillow.

To nuns, their classrooms served as protective bubbles insulating youngsters from the three Ps: pagans, Protestants, and Publics. Catholic schools were looked upon as safe houses where sisters could shield young people from worldly indiscretions like crucifix-less classrooms and cars without St. Christopher glued to their dashboards. Deportation to public school was every Catholic child's nightmare.

Lest schoolchildren mistake their Catholic-school refuge as some sort of birthright, sisters quickly pointed out those who could not do

God's will would be banished to public school. Keeping a messy desk, wasting paper, or fidgeting could send a child packing.

"Sister Raymond threatened to send me away for fidgeting. I didn't know what the word meant," Frank Dupino recalled. "Each time Sister snapped at me to stop fidgeting, I moved around in my chair, picked up my pencil, tapped my fingers. I tried anything to stop fidgeting. The more she yelled, the more I fidgeted; the more I fidgeted, the more she yelled."

Comfortable in knowing their students were protected from outside evils, sisters launched a dynamic education program, often under burdensome conditions. There were no state-mandated teacher/child ratios. One nun often taught fifty to sixty students sitting desk to desk, crammed in their classrooms like canned sardines. The only assistance came from appointed helpers—children themselves. Sisters made up for shortcomings through ingenuity, artistry, and old-fashioned know-how.

Before a sister opened a textbook, she established classroom order. With kids jam-packed in a room, potential for chaos hung over her head like a tarnished halo. Children were seated in rows, with boys on one side, girls on the other; shortest in the front, tallest in the back. Unless in use with a pencil, hands were placed either clasped together on top of the desk or palms down, resting on a lap. Movement between classrooms was wordless and synchronized, children marching in step to the *clack-clack-clack* of Sister's clicker.

With order established, sisters settled into the tough stuff—actually teaching Johnny how to read, spell, write, add, and subtract. Nuns were ahead of the education curve and among the first to implement chi-chi techniques like musical reinforcement. Decades before Kermit the Frog croaked out "African Alphabet Song," Sr. Bernadette strummed a guitar and belted out "First I Must Honor God" to impress upon children the Ten Commandments. Her cohort Sr. Mary Veronica, not having much of a voice herself, relied on technology. A 33-rpm recording of "two times two is four; two times three is six" to teach multiplication tables played daily in her classroom.

Nuns also were among the first to pioneer tactile teaching methods, emphasizing "feeling is learning." In one Catholic school during the early '60s, a young boy had difficulty learning vowel sounds. Instead of saying "ow," he said, "ooh." Sister Vincent pulled out her trusty pointer and instructed the boy to stretch out his hand, palm up.

Thwack. Down came the pointer and "ooh" squealed the boy. Again, she swatted him with the pointer, trying to pull out an "ow" instead of an "ooh." No such luck. The little boy oohed. Sister whacked again and the boy oohed. This went back and forth until he finally yelped "ow." Lesson learned.

Daily vexations sometimes took their toll, turning otherwise meek, angelic creatures into raging fiends. Tony Goodman remembers his best friend Arnie's difficulty learning how to divide fractions.

"Sister Ambrose did her best to help Arnie understand the tough math concept. She pulled out all stops, even a few that probably had Marie Montessori rolling over in her grave."

Sister Ambrose raised her voice louder and louder until she was shouting the instructions, but Arnie still couldn't get it. She resorted to one last measure: brute force.

Sister's fury erupted as she raced up the aisle to the chalkboard where Arnie, one of the largest boys in the class, stood staring at the math problems. Mustering strength that belied her four-eleven frame, the nun grabbed Arnie by his belt, picked him off the floor, and turned him upside down, screaming, "You invert! Invert! Invert!"

Although a few nuns occasionally lost it and resorted to tirades (and who wouldn't, facing sixty kids each day with no help?), most preferred encouraging youngsters in their schoolwork. With a quick prayer to St. Chrysostom, whose name is Greek for "golden mouth," nuns metamorphosed into motivational experts; Zig Ziglar and Norman Vincent Peale rolled into a single habit. Whether sharing kind thoughts or inspirational messages, nuns pulled trick after trick out of their flowing sleeves. For Sr. Mary Carol, though, setting the mood with music worked wonders.

Each morning before the school bell rang Sr. Mary Carol spun an album on a small record player hidden behind her desk and greeted students with tunes from her favorite musical group. How could Smokey and The Miracles *not* motivate a class of sixteen-year-olds in 1968?

In spite of sisters' efforts to create order and harmony, no Catholic classroom was completely free of annoyances and disturbances. However, nuns quelled uprisings before they slipped entirely of hand, often by dispatching humor.

Sister Josephine strolled up and down the aisle checking math homework and stopped at Petey McSpade's desk, Brenda Arnold Donahoe recounted. His paper was blank.

"Why, Petey, where's your work?" Donahoe recalled Sister asking the boy.

"It's right here, Sister."

"Right here? There's nothing there, Petey. Where?"

"Here, Sister," he said, pointing to a blank sheet of paper.

"But Petey, there's not a number anywhere on it," she said, jabbing the empty paper. "Where in Mary and Joseph's name is your homework?"

"It's here, on this paper. I used invisible ink."

The entire class forgot the silence-while-Sister-blows-her-stack protocol and burst into laughter. Even Sister Josephine couldn't keep a straight face.

Learning social and civic responsibility was as crucial as studying history or science. That philosophy led to educating children in an important lifelong Catholic practice—parting with their money for the good of others. Nuns were so adept at cultivating this obligation that they might have been approached by televangelists for pointers. When a preacher during the 1960s drew acclaim by issuing a plea to secure spots in heaven by sending him money, a good many Catholics might have thought he had consulted with a nun.

No matter what order they joined, all nuns turned into Sisters of Charity when it came to saving spare change for missions serving impoverished foreigners. Funding far-off missions wasn't enough in most cases. Many sisters collected money so students could ransom pagan babies—bring some lucky foreign child into the Catholic faith.

As the old saying goes, charity begins at home, and for nuns that meant raising funds for the parish. Child labor laws were set aside every fall on behalf of the local Catholic school where sisters prided themselves on beating out the Fuller Brush man. Teaching children how to sell World's Finest Chocolates was as natural to sisters as explaining how to diagram sentences. Seemingly weekly, children trotted through neighborhoods clad in starched uniforms and knocked on doors with offers of candy, nuts, magazines, and raffle tickets. Nuns stirred sales forces into action with imagination, creativity, and, as always, large doses of guilt.

Some sisters gave their charges confidence to hawk almost anything. One young nun at St. Mark's encouraged her grade-school students to peddle raffle tickets for a basket of cheer. Jimmy Pines, fourth grade's pre-eminent salesman, hit the streets with gusto, extolling benefits of cleaner, fresher smelling clothes from the laundry detergent in the basket. Winning neighborhood Bible-Belt Protestants were stunned when the neighborhood's little Willie Loman dropped off a basket of booze.

Life wasn't all work and no play in Catholic schools. A well-rounded education included exposure to the arts, at all grade levels. Trips to movies like *Ben Hur* and *The Cross and Switchblade* were instrumental in supporting sisters' history lessons or discussions on peer pressure. Visits to museums, conservatories, and musical productions were commonplace.

Topping the bill, however, were school programs. Nearly every Catholic school had its own Sr. Cecil B. DeMille, a nun whose life vocation was creating the next greatest show on earth. Sister Cecil B. specialized in Vegas-styled events, especially during the holidays. Directing hundreds of kids teetering on rickety risers as they sang the "Hallaleujah Chorus," while at the same time showing Joseph how to lead Mary and baby Jesus around on a makeshift cardboard ass, Sister created her own version of heaven on Earth. To parents agonizing through marathon performances, her vision may have seemed more like hell.

As easily as she threw together major gigs, a Sr. Cecil B. could also craft pageantry on a whim, often turning routine lessons into Broadwaywannabe productions.

"After Spanish lessons one morning, Sr. Agatha handed me a bullfighter's costume, complete with a red cape," said Tammy Hudson. "I had recently moved to the United States from Hungary and spoke very little English, and of course, no Spanish, so I really didn't know what was expected of me."

"Sister Agatha marched me up and down the hallways, stopping to visit a classroom with older students. She plopped me on top of the teacher's desk and said, 'Perform.'

"'Tora, Tora, Tora,' I yelled, stomping my feet and flipping my cap back and forth.

"The other children laughed, Sister beamed, and I smiled. I had no idea why I was leaping around in that costume. I still don't."

Sisters taught a sound body was as important as a sound mind. Practicing what they preached, sisters often hiked their skirts up over their ankles and jumped into schoolyard games. It wasn't uncommon to find a fully shrouded sister shooting hoops or jumping rope with her students, but one nun took recreation up a notch: she boxed. Sister Mary Regina hung a pair of boxing gloves on a nail in her classroom, taking them down for an occasional sparring match.

Many nuns were sports nuts who shared their passion with students. When it came to baseball, sisters were especially fervent and, true to form, rooted for the underdog. Bill Walsh remembers when the Detroit Tigers finally earned a berth in the 1968 World Series after twenty-three years of effort. After spending a summer watching pitcher phenom Denny McClain lead fellow Tigers to the championship, Walsh recalled the accomplishment as bittersweet. Since the first World Series night game was still three years away, the matchups would take place during the day when he was in school.

"St. Hugo nuns weren't about to miss out on the action, and apparently, neither would we," Walsh said.

During regular season, the nuns finagled tickets from parishioners and sailed off to Tiger Stadium in the nunmobile, the convent station wagon. When the team made it to the World Series, the sisters placed black-and-white television sets throughout the school, allowing them, and the kids, to watch their beloved Tigers beat the Cardinals for the title.

Even though nuns mostly were secluded from the world (save for a trip to the ballpark), that didn't stop them from bringing the world to their students. Every nun since the early twentieth century had taught children to pray for the conversion of Russia and the downfall of Communism, opening the door to discussing global politics—all without the aid of television, satellites, or the World Wide Web.

Nuns, even those born outside of the United States, taught children the importance of patriotism, sometimes when society suggested otherwise. Martin Golbrowski recalls the turmoil sweeping the nation in 1966 when the United States was embroiled in the Vietnam War. Troops fought an enemy on a continent halfway around the world while antiwar protestors took their battle to homeland streets. For Golbrowski, then a sixth grader, times were confusing. To his teacher, Sr. Jane de Chantal, there was no confusion.

"Sister had been a very young woman during World War I; she grew older and wiser throughout World War II and the Korean Conflict. As Vietnam battles raged on, she knew where to direct our thoughts," Golbrowski said.

For that year's Christmas pageant, Sister saw to it the children all wore matching green berets and sang "The Ballad of The Green Berets" for the show's finale. The astute woman accomplished a task so few could that year: masterminded a rousing show of patriotism.

As children passed from grade to grade, trading in Sr. Mary Rose for Sr. Isabel and Sr. Isabel for Sr. Therese, they no longer feared threats of "off to school with the Publics you go." By then, kids were smart enough to realize their public-school friends had half as much homework and talked to each other when they ate lunch or when they walked the hallways. In fact, some kids actually begged their parents to send them off to school with Publics. They knew better than to tell the nuns, though. Years later, it turns out most were glad they stayed.

EDUCATION MEMORIES

Inside the Classroom: 3Rs ... English, Latin, and French, Too

Latin Hummingbirds

In Latin class we were learning the *Confiteor*, one of the prayers that all altar boys were required to know. Both the language and the prayer had a lilting, musical quality to them. A few of us guys figured that since everyone was saying it together, we would just hum along. Sister Leo wouldn't know the difference.

One morning Sister announced to the class, "Tomorrow we are having a guest group so we'll have an 'off-day' in Latin class." The class was ecstatic. No work!

The following day, Sister Leo introduced the group to the class: the hummingbirds. I looked around but didn't see anyone other than my classmates. Sister then asked my buddies and me to come to the front of the room where we were instructed to hum Latin for our classmates.

Spelling-Bee Fiasco

When it came to be my turn in the fourth-grade spelling bee, I was given the word "fort." I spelled f-a-r-t and said "fort." Sister turned red and asked me to spell it again. This time I spelled f-o-r-t but said "fart." The look on her face nearly drove me to shame.

Hit Those Notes, Not Me

Our music teacher, Sr. Mary Therese, had an "inspirational" way of encouraging us to reach high notes. "Higher, higher, higher," she said, slapping us under our chins each time she said "higher." She kept this up until we sang high enough to appease her. Unfortunately for me, I sang alto and needed lots of "encouragement" to reach those high notes.

Dashed Singing Career

I was in choir, singing my heart out. Sister stood directly in front of me for a few minutes, listening intently to my warbling.

"You really can't carry a tune, you know," Sister said.

Shattered, I stopped singing for a long time. To this day I still find it hard to do.

Parlez-Vous Français?

My first few days in Sr. Henrietta's class were strange, to say the least. Sister was French-Canadian and French was her native language. When I entered the class as a new student she introduced me to the other kids and then spoke to me in French. I didn't understand a word she said.

Sister started each morning with instructions to the class, covering our lessons for the day. First, she spoke to the entire class in English, and then turned to me and spoke French. She liked to ask me questions in French, too, but she always translated them into English for the benefit of the rest of the class. I could always figure out what she was saying because of her translations.

One morning, she spoke to me in French. This time, she didn't translate. She repeated herself when I didn't respond. Finally, she asked me, "Parlez-vous Français?" I shook my head no.

"Not French?" she asked in English.

Again, I shook my head no.

Sister laughed and explained to me that since she and I shared the same last name—Toussaint—she assumed we both shared the same native tongue.

She's No Singing Nun

My second-grade teacher's method for judging our singing abilities was quite intimidating. Sister Theopilia strolled up and down the rows of desks, stopped at each one, and instructed each of us to stand and sing. No music, no accompaniment, just seven-year-old soloists singing a cappella.

After listening to us, she went back to her desk and recorded our grades. Having sister hover over me while I sang turned me into a nervous wreck! I never earned a grade higher than a B. Adding insult to injury was the fact Sister couldn't carry a tune in a bucket.

Hey, John, Is That You?

My sophomore year was a tough one, due mostly to my difficulties with my English teacher, Sr. Gregory. Each day was pure torture. I was certain she hated me. I could do nothing right. Eventually, the year ended and I moved up a grade.

After the first three weeks of my junior year my English teacher became ill and stopped teaching. The following week we were greeted with a new teacher. To my utter horror, it was Sr. Gregory. She welcomed the class and then took roll, calling out each of our names.

"John. John?"

No answer.

"John Findley?" Sr. Gregory continued, looking around the room.

My name was next on the roll but it is Richard, not John. I looked around the room for "John" when a friend whispered, "I think she's talking to you!"

"Present." I wasn't about to correct her.

"Welcome to the class, John. I'm sure we'll have a very good year," she said and then asked me to run an errand to the office.

From that moment forward I became John, the fair-haired boy who could do no wrong. By the end of that first week with Sr. Gregory, even my fellow classmates and faculty members who remembered my terrible sophomore year were calling me John.

That was my best year ever; I even learned what it meant to be a teacher's pet. I left at the end of the school year never telling the good sister her mistake. God works in wonderful ways and, sometimes, very quickly.

Pump That Organ

My music teacher, Sr. Evangeline, was tiny. Her feet couldn't reach the piano pedals. Since I was a little guy, I became her teacher's pet, in a strange way. Sister assigned me the special job of crouching underneath the piano and pushing the pedals while she played the keyboard. If I lagged behind, Sr. Evangeline tapped me on my bottom a couple of times as a reminder to pick up the pace.

Double Trouble

I was looking forward to my junior year and attending our ring dance, driving, gaining independence, and enjoying being a typical sixteen-year-old. All was great. Except for chemistry, that is. Sister Mary Veronica, a tall, strong, and rugged-looking Irish nun who wore gold-rimmed glasses, taught the class. She was an excellent instructor, patient and caring but firm. Nevertheless, she intimidated me because chemistry was not one of my favorite subjects.

I did fairly well in the subject, scoring in the low-to-mid eighties on tests. However, when I received my first-quarter report card, my average was eighty-nine. Delighted with the grade, I never questioned it. The second quarter came around with the same happy result.

One day during lab, Sr. Mary Veronica summoned my attention with an unusual question: "Miss Salimbene, why do you sign your name 'Catherine' one day and 'Angela' the next?"

All thirty of my classmates stared at little ol' quiet me while my heart nearly stopped. I was never in trouble. Incredulous, I asked, "What?"

"Come to my desk *now!*"

As I hurried out of my seat, I wondered how I could have done such a thing. Sister showed me evidence. In her left hand was neatly written homework with my flowery signature. In her right hand was another sheet of painstakingly scribed work—penned in the flowery signature of my *twin sister*, Angela.

"Sister, the handwriting is different in these. One is mine, the other is my sister's."

Sister's normally cherubic face turned a bright, burning red. Sister's anger had me thinking maybe I actually *had* signed Angela's name by mistake. I never considered the possibility that Sister didn't realize there were two of us. Remember, nuns were always right.

Sister Storm Trooper

By the time I had Sr. Kathleen in the late '90s, she was *very* old. She liked drawing comparisons to Star Wars movies in her lessons. She talked about Luke Skywalker, telling us he walked in Christ. Before becoming a nun Sr. Kathleen was a state trooper. I guess she had a personal connection to storm troopers as well.

Cold Germs
Sister kept the classroom icy cold and we couldn't wear jackets inside, only sweaters. She told us germs travel around but not when it was cold, so she kept the temperature low.

Holy God, We Praise Thy Name
Each Wednesday the entire student body attended benediction, where we prayed and sang songs. Included in the song list was "Holy God, We Praise Thy Name," which at that time was one of my favorites. In one part of the song, we were to sing the word "scepter"—pronounced "septer." Of course, the collective diction of 300 young schoolchildren, most yearning to get out of church, wasn't exactly in top form. Our voices rang out a resounding "septcher."

Sister Stella would have none of that! We remained in our seats singing the line over and over again, until all of us pronounced the word correctly. Some days we stayed there for hours, almost until lunchtime. Assuredly, as I sing that song today, I take exceptional pains to pronounce the word "scepter" clear enough that even Sr. Stella in heaven can understand me.

Beyond the Classroom: Enrichment and Extension

Arbor Day
Arbor Day wasn't the celebrated holiday back in the '30s that it is today. But Sr. Mary Thomas thought it should be. What better way to see God's handiwork, she reasoned, than planting a tree and watching it grow? To demonstrate her point, Sister led us each spring into the glen, a forested portion of the property on which the school was located. There, she created an informal botany lesson where we observed and reveled in God's gift of beauty to us.

Trilingual Education

In grade school I was taught by Filippini nuns from Italy who believed that learning to speak Italian went hand in hand with our religious education. So, not only was I required to learn my prayers in English and Latin, but Italian, too. Thinking back, I'm astounded that we little children were trilingual!

Whirling Dervish

Sister Mary Peter was a ten-year-old Irish lass wrapped up in the body of a sixty-four-year-old woman wearing an old gray habit. Her vocabulary lessons wandered from explaining definitions to sharing stories of her childhood encounters with a leprechaun named Seamus.

One afternoon as she drifted back to the Emerald Isle, Sister abruptly decided her class should be introduced to the Irish jig. She stood in front of the class and demonstrated the ancient Gaelic dance. One by one we were called to the front of the room where our classmates graded us. Those performing the jig well were allowed early dismissal. Those who had not, stayed behind to practice.

Since I was a standout athlete in several sports, and with the last name Devlin, obviously of Irish heritage, I was a lock to be one of those granted early release. Or so I assumed. Several girls quickly exited after dancing the simple step-bounce-step-kick routine. Then a few of the guys gave it a try with a couple gaining early release and a few staying behind.

My turn came and I was ready. I had written down that night's assignment and my books were packed for dismissal so I raced to the front of the room.

"Ah, James Patrick, I was wondering how long before you decided to represent your clan," Sr. Mary Peter said while I stretched and hopped around in mock calisthenics.

I was ready. *Kick, jump, step, turn step, kick, jump, jump.* After the laughter subsided, I threw a look of confidence to Sr. Mary Peter and headed toward the door.

"No dear! No, no, no, NO!" Sister said, her hands folded in front of her and head shaking vigorously from side to side. "You are a whirling dervish, not a Devlin!

"I only pray that St. Patrick did not bear witness to that display."

The now much louder laughter echoed down the hallway when Sr. Mary Peter handed me the pink after-school detention form.

Diversion and Disruptions in the Classroom: Breaks in the Lesson Plan

Rockin' Sockin' Sister

Terror marked my first day in the seventh grade. I had been assigned to the homeroom of Sr. Mary Regina, the only nun in our school with boxing gloves hanging on her pencil sharpener.

Just as the Irish would describe her, Sr. Mary Regina was a "stout" woman, of average height. As the year wore on, I never saw her use the gloves. That is, not until the day Tom Silvers came to visit.

Tom was in high school but had been in Sr. Mary Regina's class when he was younger. A funny and engaging boy, Tom was the class clown whom trouble always found. According to my older brother, who also had been in Sr. Mary Regina's class, Tom was such a funny character that he never could anger Sister. In fact, Sister and Tom jokingly sparred with each other.

One afternoon on a day the high school was closed, Tom appeared outside our classroom and challenged Sister to a friendly boxing match. She grabbed her gloves off the pencil sharpener and stepped into the hallway with a warning for us to quietly finish our work. Of course, none of us touched our work! We were too busy listening to the commotion in the hallway.

The pretend pugilists stayed out of our line of vision until a black headdress and veil flew by the doorway. Immediately, Sr. Mary Regina followed in pursuit, exposing her hair. We were astonished. None of us had ever seen a nun's hair. Hers was short and graying, pressed back in a way that made me wonder if Sister had stepped in a wind tunnel each morning before dressing.

Once again, Sister was out of our line of sight, but we still could hear her chasing Tom as he ran out of the building laughing. Sister Mary Regina stepped back into the classroom, habit in place, and began teaching us as if nothing had happened. However, the match remains forever etched in my mind.

I Don't Care Who You Are, Read!

Well past her teaching prime, my eighth-grade history teacher Sr. Mary Thomas usually called students anything but their given names. One morning we were taking turns reading aloud from the text when Sister called my name, indicating my turn to read. When I lifted my head in acknowledgement, I noticed Sr. Mary Thomas staring at my friend Charlie, two rows over.

"Joseph," Sister said again, looking at Charlie. Charlie didn't raise his head.

"Joseph?" She called my name a third time but by now she was striding toward Charlie, who still hadn't raised his head.

Reaching his desk before Charlie had a chance to see what was coming, Sister smacked him on the head with her book while yelling at him, "Joseph, I told you to read!"

"Sister Mary Thomas, I'm not Joseph," a shocked and dazed Charlie cried out.

"I don't care who you are, I told you to read!"

Sister's religious order? The Sisters of Mercy, naturally.

World Travelers

Our fifth-grade class gave Sr. Hubert a talking globe for Christmas. Not long afterward, she placed us one by one in the closet with the globe. Take a trip around the world, she told us. About all I got out of that travel was claustrophobia!

Mouse Attack

A mouse entered our classroom through an open pipe in the wall. Sister spotted the rodent and hopped on her desk, hollering at us to help her. All we could do was laugh.

Don't Fly Away!

Some of us students in Sr. John Marie's writing class saw a pigeon resting on the window ledge and tried scaring it away. Sister had a fit, claiming that the bird might be the Holy Ghost. She was such a sweet lady, although a little nutty.

Kleptomaniac Teacher's Pet

Marty was the quintessential teacher's pet. With his hand shooting up in the air flagging attention, he brown-nosed Sister with offers of "May I help you with that, Sister?" "I'd be happy to take care of that, Sister." He easily charmed his way into teacher's pet status.

Sister always counted on Marty staying behind to clean chalkboards. At first we thought he had a chalk fetish but soon learned his volunteerism was driven by ulterior motives. He was a thief.

As soon as Sister cleared the classroom and left Marty alone, the young kleptomaniac rifled through her desk, stashing holy cards, small statues, and other religious trinkets into his pockets.

Marty never was caught, not even after he wrapped the stolen goods and gave them back to the nuns as gifts a few years later.

Laugh Your Donkey Off

It was a beautiful spring day so Sister threw open the windows to let in fresh air. Along came a donkey just outside our windows. It brayed *eeeh awww, eeeh awww*. We children laughed our heads off! Sister let us know how disgusted she was with our outburst. We turned silent. Her parting words on the subject? "And he came into his own and his own received him not."

Classroom Order: Rules and Procedures

Fingertips of Silence

The sisters did not allow us to talk in class, in the hallways, or outside in the bus pickup line. Every time we left our classrooms we were required to place one of our index fingers on our lips as a silent reminder to each other not to talk.

How Loud Do You Want to Speak, Sister?

Our honors English teacher Sister Mary Rose used a microphone to address our class the first day of school. She explained the microphone was necessary because she had throat cancer and would probably speak too softly for us to hear. Although we were touched by her circumstances, we couldn't help but be amused. The microphone was never plugged in and we heard her just fine!

I Want That in Duplicate

From the moment we stepped into Sr. Cabrini's Spanish class our senior year, my classmates and I knew it wasn't going to be a cakewalk. Our three-year track record in Spanish hadn't exactly inspired Sister's confidence in our capabilities. She ordered us to write all our lessons, test answers, and homework in a spiral-bound notebook with perforated edges. Use carbon paper, too, she instructed.

"I have a copy and you have a copy. If you have questions about your grades, we will then refer back to the answers we both have."

This eliminated any temptation we might have had to change or modify our responses after she graded the class work. This must have been a prevailing problem because Sr. Cabrini instituted the carbon-copy policy in all her classes. I wonder what tactic she would use in our carbonless world today.

Short Stuff

I was the shortest child in my first-grade class. Since the nuns always lined us up from shortest to tallest for single-file marches through the hallways, I always was the lead student, right behind Sister. Unfortunately for Sister, I also was the least observant. Without fail, whenever Sister stopped I continued moving, plowing into her and losing myself in the folds of her skirt.

Goosestepping

The sisters always marched us into church in two rows, with partners almost elbow to elbow. With our heads bowed and hands clasped in reverence, we walked together in a unified step. Once the two lead girls reached their pew, Sister snapped a rubber band attached to her prayer book, signaling all of us to kneel in genuflection at the same time. Sister snapped the band again and we rose in unison. Nuns were orderly creatures, that's for sure.

Which Door Was That, Monty?

Sister Clement Mark asked me to carry a note to the teacher in my older sister's class. When I delivered it I was in a hurry to get out of the room unnoticed. I walked out the wrong door and into the coatroom. I even closed the door behind me. What a jolt to look around and see jackets and coats instead of an open hallway. As peals of laughter rang out behind me, all I could think of was going back into that classroom in front of those older kids. After that day, I prayed Sr. Clement Mark wouldn't call on me again to deliver messages. She never did.

Rosary Beads Terror

The good Sister walked up and down each row of seats while we prayed the rosary. When Sister stood next to a desk, the student seated there needed to tell her which mystery was being prayed. When students couldn't answer, it meant either they weren't paying attention or, worse yet, they had forgotten their rosary beads.

She stood next to my desk and as I prayed *Hail Mary, full of grace*, I glanced upward. Mistake! She was staring at my hands. Her mouth twisted and her eyes shifted. Sister was ready for battle. My brain screamed pleas for help that no one would hear.

"Where are your rosary beads, missy?"

I threw my hands over my head and figured it was time to speak fast, with complete assurance that Sister would believe whatever I told her.

"Get your hands off your hand and answer me, you bold and brazen article, you."

Words started streaming out of my mouth. Unfortunately my brain didn't have anything to do with them.

"Sister, I'm sorry. I must have left them at home, lunchtime, on the table in the kitchen where I was eating my sandwich. It was tuna, of course, because today is Friday and I never eat meat on Friday because that is a sin. I had my beads in my hands because I was praying, like I do all the time. My mom told me to hurry up or I'd be late. Just then, my little brother threw up because he ate something."

What the hell was I saying? The words were flying out of my mouth.

"Maybe it was a crayon? It looked blue. I couldn't finish my lunch because I wanted to continue praying but I hadn't finished my sandwich so I asked myself, 'What would Sister do? Finish her lunch or keep praying?' My mother yelled for me to get going and I ran out the door. Look at my bruised knee and elbow! I fell trying to hurry so as not to be late because I know you hate for us to be late and...."

"*Hold your tongue!*" Sister bellowed. I had no clue what I had just told her.

Sister's mouth twisted again and her eyes squinted. She looked just like someone who couldn't read the last line on an eye-exam chart.

"You are a bold and brazen child. Step to the rear of the classroom." I did, of course. The class continued praying the rosary but I knew full well she wasn't finished with me. After she completed the prayer, Sister approached me and grabbed my hands off my head.

"Class, stand," she directed the rest of the students. "Take your hands off your heads. What's wrong with you people? Turn and face the rear of the room.

"The devil made her forget her rosary beads and if she gets into an accident, who will know to summon a priest? If she dies without seeing a priest, the devil will take her soul immediately to hell.

"See these hanging from my side?" Sister asked, fondling the beads hanging from her belt. "*These* are my ticket to heaven."

I had to remain in the back of the room for the rest of the day, my rosaryless hands tucked into my pockets. Some good did come from my terror. My classmates and I discovered if we cut about six inches from a set of beads we would have enough to wrap around our fingers and look as if the rest of the beads were tucked in closed fists. Each day after lunch we'd check the lines of girls with faces drawn in terror, their eyes staring blankly and lips quivering. Those girls had forgotten their rosaries. If we had enough left on our beads—charity begins at home, after all—we'd cut off a bit and share.

Sister was happy, we were happy, and the school store sold more rosaries that year.

The Maestro

Sister Mary Alice was a great nun. She often kept our attention by climbing on top of her desk to conduct class.

Outside the Classroom: Recess, Recreation, and Routines

Just Hanging Around

I started school cold turkey in the first grade. Other than an occasional dance lesson, I had never spent any time away from home. I was petrified.

My older sister took me by the hand and was instructed to walk me to my classroom. As soon as we reached the school grounds, Beth met up with her friends and left me in the dust. She pointed to my classroom and took off.

Terrified, I didn't go to the room. I just hid out in the schoolyard. When the children came out for recess, I ran around like they did. When they ate their lunch, I ate mine. I kept up this charade for three days. The days were long but I figured they were much better than the alternative.

Finally, a teacher discovered me and escorted me to Sr. Monica, the most feared sister at St. Mary Magdalene's. I was labeled a troublemaker and sentenced to Sr. Monica's classroom for the year. Ironically, had I entered the classroom pointed out to me the first day, I would have been treated to a kind and sweet lay teacher.

Cole Slaw Carol

Carol was the prettiest girl in the second grade and I had a crush on her. Imagine how excited I was when she sat next to me in the cafeteria at lunchtime.

The sisters had a rule that if we didn't eat our entire lunch, we weren't allowed to go outside. That day, we were served cole slaw. No one liked cole slaw. It was served with a jellybean on top in a weak attempt to mask what lay underneath. It was still cole slaw.

Turning to Carol, I pushed the slaw away and said, "I'm not eating this!"

"I'm not eating it either," she agreed, shoving her slaw away.

I couldn't believe it! The pretty, popular girl supported me. I started feeling sorry for her, knowing she would miss recess—all because of me. I suggested we cry.

On cue, both of us sobbed, releasing crocodile tears in the hopes of eliciting pity from Sr. Magdalene. Carol also pretended to eat the slaw, pushing the mush around her plate. Actually, she ate only the jellybean. Sister issued her a reprieve. Carol happily skipped out of the cafeteria on her way to recess. Without me.

I was not pardoned. After sitting in front of that slop for nearly a half hour, through lunch and recess, I pitched a fit. I threw my cole slaw into the trash can and stormed out of the room. After digging out my lunch and putting it back on my plate, Sr. Magdalene dragged me back to the cafeteria and tried forcing me to finish lunch. I still wouldn't eat it. I sat at that table, slaw in front of me, until dismissal.

Hot-Dog Day

Our parish was young and growing during the early '60s. Amenities like cafeterias were nonexistent, so our children brought lunches from home. The church had a small kitchen in the back of the social hall where the nuns eventually offered a hot-dog lunch one day a week. Since I had a large family, I enjoyed not having to pack six lunches, if only for one day a week.

Along with the establishment of Hot-Dog Day, the nuns put into place an order-taking system based on color-coded tickets. A red ticket meant only ketchup on the dog; a yellow for mustard; green for combination mustard and ketchup; and white for plain.

One Hot-Dog Day afternoon, I received a phone call from Sr. Agatha, the school's music teacher.

"I'm sorry to tell you but I found a hot dog hidden in the record player," Sister reported. "When the children order hot dogs, they are expected to eat them."

"OK," I answered, wondering why she was telling me all this.

"The hot dog belonged to Shannon," she said, referring to one of my daughters.

"Are you sure?" There were hundreds of children attending the school.

"The hot dog was a 'combination.' Shannon was the only one in her class to order a combination," Sister explained. Drawing a mental picture of Sr. Agatha inspecting a smooshed hot dog lathered in mustard and ketchup, and then cross-referencing the evidence with a couple hundred orders, had me stifling laughs.

I always wondered if Sister found more hidden dogs in the weeks to come because the school soon replaced Hot-Dog Day with Hamburger Day. The burgers came from a fast-food restaurant with no mustard or ketchup on them, just pickles.

After the Classroom: Still More to Learn

Where's Your Homework?
Forgetting to have his homework signed by a parent the night before, my best friend faced "Little Joe" with a good deal of apprehension. Despite her diminutive frame—hence the nickname "Little Joe"—our fifth-grade nun managed to invoke fear in us at the slightest wrongdoing. However, this time my friend was prepared.

"Sister, I gave my homework to my mother this morning while she was fixing breakfast. She must have been too busy to sign it," he said.

"How dare you wait until the last moment to bother your dear mother, especially while she was so busy cooking bacon and spinach for you?"

I'm not sure Sister really heard herself saying those words but the rest of the class did. Bacon and spinach for breakfast?

Class Favorites

One of my nuns loved the football players in my high school. Sister Margaret Francis would do whatever it took to get them through school, including extra help in class and tutoring afterward. The rest of us had to get by on our own.

World's Finest Chocolates or Latin

Sister Albert must have disliked teaching Latin as much as we hated studying it. Either that or she was a closet chocoholic. Each year, St. Joseph High School sponsored the long-honored fund-raising tradition among Catholic schools in the 1960s—sales of World's Finest Chocolate Bars.

Kicking off the sale, Sr. Albert offered us a bribe. She promised no Latin lessons for the day if our class bought forty candy bars, at twenty-five cents each. What a deal! What a smart nun, too. There just so happened to be forty students in that class, and daily lunch cost twenty-five cents. For the next couple of weeks we all ate chocolate lunches and skipped Latin.

The best part is we sold the most candy bars and celebrated with a pizza party. Finally, no more chocolate lunches.

Money Laundering

Sister Columba was in charge of collecting all the money we raised from selling candy bars and other fund-raising items during the year. She was a bit quirky about handling the money, though. Sister required us to wash dirty dollar bills with soap and water in the school bathroom and then hang the wet bills on the radiator to dry.

Evidently she carried this compulsion over to her home life as well. Sometimes when I passed by the convent, I saw dollar bills hanging on the clothesline.

Sandwich Sales

When I was a little girl the nuns were pretty much on their own to generate funds to operate the school. Tuition was only three dollars a month, and music lessons brought in an additional five dollars per student. Clearly, that wasn't enough money to pay all the bills.

Under the sisters' direction, children from the school traveled door to door selling sandwiches made by the nuns in an effort to raise funds. The children didn't tell their customers why they were selling the sandwiches, but my grandmother instinctively knew. She always purchased sandwiches from the children, whether she needed them or not.

The Bigger Classroom: Social and Civic Lessons

A National Treasure Falls

That fall morning, decades ago, a knock on the door interrupted our class.

"A terrible tragedy has befallen us all," Sr. Mary Gertrude, our principal, said. "Hurry to the church immediately."

The response was automatic. Silently, and in a single line, we joined similar lines of students pouring out of their classrooms, all heading in the same direction. It was a somber march. The crestfallen, tear-stained faces of our nuns spoke to the magnitude of the calamity. Yet, none of them uttered a word.

Once in the church, kneeling in our pews, the principal spoke:

"We have lost our president. Pray for us all."

It was November 22, 1963. An assassin's bullet had taken the life of John F. Kennedy.

Sometimes I think nuns were put on earth to make amends for Eve's apple splurge in the Garden of Eden. No forbidden fruit for us, they taught. Avoid sin by keeping your bodies clean and holy, sisters harped. Nuns were effective. "Chaste and pure, chaste and pure" turned into a mantra, rolling around inside my head every time temptation slithered in my direction. So I never smoked, drank, took drugs, or had sex. In fact, the closest I ever came to that serpent was a pair of snakeskin mules I lusted after and bought for myself. As I'm now a [married] mother of three who enjoys an occasional merlot, I obviously slipped in later years.

D. S.

Our nuns began their patented "private parts" lectures just prior to my reaching the dreaded age of reason: seven years old. While the sisters never mentioned parts by name, all of us eventually caught on—and then depression set in. To paraphrase Humphrey Bogart in *Casablanca*, "of all the places in all the spots...."

Some of the kids discussed whether the sisters actually had private parts or, instead, were specially made, sort of like older siblings who never got their wisdom teeth. Personally, I didn't want to go there. I was still trying to get comfortable with the sisters having ears and hair.

M. P.

Chapter Four

*Private Parts
and Impure Thoughts:
Avoiding Occasions of Sins*

S ISTER RITA HANDLED SEX EDUCATION the way she taught so many other Catholic lessons: telling kids to pray. She had a system in place, too. Girls were handed St. Agnes of Rome holy cards and instructed to pray to that patron saint of virgins.

Each boy was urged to turn to St. Agatha, patron saint of volcanic eruptions. Sister gave them a holy card depicting a tortured, pious-looking slip of a girl gazing heavenward holding a pair of pliers. She hid in her drawer the version showing a stubborn, gutsy young lass having her breasts lopped off by jeering soldiers.

"These chaste women avoided relations," Sister said, carefully avoiding the s-e-x word. "They remained virgins for Jesus, undergoing humiliation, torture, and martyrdom."

"Pray you walk the same path."

Like so much else, Catholic nuns handled the lion's share of shaping children's morality. They guided children into adulthoods free from grave transgressions like murder, thievery, and calling nuns "miss" in error.

Nuns embarked on a zealous mission to ensure that young bodies and minds remained pure vestibules, clean houses in which Jesus could reside. They followed an unwritten code denouncing anything that might defile a child's body. That meant any offense against the flesh, including those only conceived and not actually carried out.

In their quest to produce moral adults, sisters plowed through a litany of sins. To twenty-first-century eyes viewing crotch-grabbing, boob-popping "reality" entertainment, the nuns' ideas of debauchery seems tame. Whether it was young ladies exposing their calves or wearing nail polish or boys flapping untucked shirts, nuns saw such indiscretions as the first domino dropping in a chain of events ending in carnal desecration. No telling where one habitual shirttail offender in Atlanta would have ended if he hadn't been humiliated out of his untidy habit in the seventh grade. Sister yanked him out of line and used her own hand to tuck in his shirt—front, back, and sides. That was the last time his shirttail hung loose.

Topping the list of sins to avoid was sex. Although this seems pretty obvious, to nuns it wasn't quite that simple because of the wide range of sexual activities tempting kids. For starters, kissing, touching, lusting, or *just thinking about* kissing, touching, and lusting were violations. In fact, merely hanging out or talking with someone of the opposite sex could draw out the veiled morality police.

For Peter Smithton, trying to assist a fellow student pegged him as a thirteen-year-old deviant.

"Some of the girls were standing in the grassy area talking when one of them noticed she had lost her earring," Smithton said.

With an offer to help search, Smithton got down on his hands and knees and combed the grass for the missing jewelry while the girls clustered nearby. He had barely gotten down on all fours when a violent tug on his shirt jerked him to his feet.

"You'll not be looking up girls' dresses in my school," shrieked Sr. Boniface.

"I won't have a pervert here at St. Ignatius, no I won't," she screamed, ignoring Smithton's and the girls' insistence he was only looking for the earring.

Considering the extremely limited knowledge most of these women had on the subject of sex, advice and guidelines were vague and often cloaked in euphemisms. Several women from different cities recalled hearing the same recommendation for traveling in cars with boys. Bring along a pillow, several nuns suggested, so if the young lady needed to sit on a boy's lap, she could place it between herself and the boy.

One area many nuns *did* feel comfortable discussing was "private parts." Never actually describing which parts of the body were private, sisters forged on with discussions that, after cautioning children to not touch their intimates, centered on protecting their holy bits by keeping them hidden.

Instead of waiting for an all-out morality war to erupt, nuns initiated pre-emptive strikes: inspections. Carried out with the diligence of white-gloved boot camp drill instructors, nuns scrutinized students from head to toe in search of virtue violations. Nearly every woman taught by a nun recalls hem checks—kneeling on the floor so Sister could see the skirt touching the floor, an assurance girls were modestly covered.

Just as a good drill sergeant followed up barracks inspections with a check of the head, nuns examined all sorts of clothing, including slips and bras.

Sister Felicity at Villa Cabrini Academy believed only bold girls wore bras before they needed them. Every morning she stood outside the classroom doorway and greeted each girl with a welcoming pat on the shoulder. Sister actually was groping for bra straps, a subtle action that went unnoticed by other students, explained former student Karen Michaels. Sister Felicity marched offenders to the bathroom and ordered them to remove their bras. Pity the poor girls who matured early.

In search of potential violators, sisters often went on reconnaissance, patrolling church-going procession lines, playground jungle gyms, and, especially, teen dances. These hunts were so widespread that students swore nuns formed NAPS—Nuns Against Perverted Students.

An all-girl high school in Pittsburgh occasionally teamed up with an all-boy school for dances. The gym remained well lit while nuns glided around the room, separating boys and girls dancing less than an arm's length away, a former student remembered.

"As we danced and they cruised among us, sisters told us to pray an Our Father and Hail Mary for protection from our dancing partner," Barbara Parker said.

"As if that would help."

Some nuns tried doling out sex-related advice to girls. Most of it was ambiguous, naïve, and sometimes untrue. Several women remembered being counseled to avoid wearing certain colors: white because it would remind boys of a bedsheet and red because it evoked passion. Other times, sisters didn't mince words: French kissing was the equivalent of mini-intercourse, one nun warned her girls.

Sisters often were called upon to dispense reproduction details. This rattled some nuns, particularly when it meant giving "the talk" to young girls. In fact, one sister teaching a group of girls menstruation facts readied them as if they were in the midst of a World War II air raid, blackening the windows with cardboard so the "enemy"—the boys—couldn't peek.

Many sisters believed the best way to create chaste children was helping them avoid any and all near occasions of sin. Of course, the simplest way was separating boys from girls. Even as times changed during the late '60s, a nun's vigilance did not.

"Our classes were segregated by sex; boys on one side of the building, girls on another," Sheila Rooney recounted. "It wasn't until my junior year we were even allowed to eat lunch together. By that time, for all we girls knew, sitting next to a boy in the cafeteria was one step away from becoming pregnant."

At St. Clare's all-girl high school in Woonsocket, Rhode Island, nuns made sure no one crossed the line—literally. The sisters had staked out boundaries in the schoolyard, about ten feet away from the street, where the boys cruised by each day during lunchtime.

"If we slowed down to talk to the girls, a nun standing on the sidewalk with a clipboard in her hand wrote down our license plate numbers and 'turned us in.' The brothers had a good laugh over that one," reminisced Richard Laferriere.

Sex may have been on the top of the list of sins to avoid, but poor hygiene was probably the one that dropped most nuns to their knees in novenas. Never truer was the claim "cleanliness is next to Godliness" than in a class taught by a nun. Inspecting young hands, fingernails, and hair for dirt, polish, and critters was as much a part of classroom routine as kneeling in morning prayer for twenty minutes each day.

"I thought dangling my long hair in my face made me look cool," recalled Anna Archer. "Sister Mary John did not. She waved a pair of scissors in front of me and threatened to cut my hair herself.

"God only knows what my hair would have looked like had Sister cut it. I went home crying to my mother, begging her to buy hair clips." Her mother complied and Archer wore them in her hair the next day and every day for the rest of the school year.

Kathy Cramer remembers the "DA" haircut rage for boys during the early '60s. Nuns forbade boys from wearing the cool style—not because wings of hair overlapped from the sides of their heads to the back but because "DA" stood for "duck's ass."

Smoking, drinking, drugs, and the decimation these outside influences could bring on Catholic bodies deeply concerned nuns. Do you think Jesus wants to rest in a smoke-filled room, one nun queried? Mustering up the ire of St. Patrick banishing snakes from Ireland, some nuns resorted to extreme measures. Although unheard of today, nuns routinely barged into the boys' bathroom searching for young men with cigarettes hanging from their mouths.

One innovative nun frightened by increasing drug use during the late '60s brought in the cavalry. Each year, Sister Penelope turned over her seventh- and eighth-grade students to a wisecracking, hippie vice-cop for support. He described the evils of reefer madness and even threw in a couple of LSD flashback stories for good measure. Sister stood in a corner with her arms crossed and a smug see-what-will-happen-to-you expression plastered on her face. Officer Mod Squad's most memorable piece of advice was telling youngsters to avoid eating morning glory seeds as they "sailed you to seventh heaven." The upshot? Kids spent the afternoon harvesting the playground for morning glories.

As driven as they were in teaching students religious practices and academics, nuns were just as purposeful in helping develop a strong moral foundation in Catholic children. Generally, these women influenced young lives during a time when chastity in marriage was a virtue. Television parents like Laura and Rob slept in separate beds and Lucy wasn't "pregnant" but "expecting." Despite their doe-eyed perspective on all things carnal, sisters maintained a healthy level of distrust, which they tried to pass along to their students.

Nuns' commitment to create spiritually and physically chaste children of God most likely came from a sincere desire to save souls from hell's fire. Or maybe it was because they were driven by a fear of the unknown. One woman suggested sisters might have been envious, for certainly under the layers and folds in their habits hid their own private parts, perhaps long-forgotten. Most former students don't buy that theory, though. Many still are in therapy over discovering nuns have legs, necks, and hair.

Whatever the reason, nuns saw a battle looming over their students' virtue. As God's infantrymen, they gladly took up arms in the march for morality.

As Socrates once said, "Wars and revolutions and battles are due simply and solely to the body and its desires." Socrates must have been under the influence of a nun.

CHASTITY, PURITY, AND REMAINING SINLESS MEMORIES

Avoiding Sin: Following Sister's Advice

Shop This Way
The nuns instructed us boys to avoid specific aisles in the drugstore so as not to be tempted by certain magazines. This was before the days when *Hustler* or *Penthouse* appeared on store shelves willy nilly, and

before the Legion of Decency prevailed on shopkeepers to use brown paper to cover *Esquire*.

Sister Slap

I was a twenty-two-year-old serviceman, home on leave from Korea for a few weeks, when I ran into one of my buddies. He was dating a young lady who had a single sister.

"Up for a double date?"

I knew the girl. She married at eighteen and divorced at twenty. She was very attractive, too. I didn't see any harm in a date.

"Sure, why not?"

That was Tuesday and the date was set for Saturday. Thursday, I received a phone call from Sr. Anna, a delightfully warm and compassionate woman. She had been one of my favorite nuns at school. Sister Anna invited me to stop by for a visit.

Sister led me through the hallways to her office, not saying a word. Once in her office, with steely eyes boring through me, she finally spoke:

"I hear you're going out with Maureen Abbott."

"Yeah, I was thinking about it."

Sister pulled back her hand as if she were pulling the string on an archer's bow and—*whack*—smacked me across the face with the palm of her hand. How it stung! She really laid one on me. She never said another word. Both my face and pride smarted.

I wasn't sure why Sister Anna slapped me. Maybe she thought I would commit some unspeakable sin by dating a divorced woman. Or worse, I might marry the woman and send us both to hell. It didn't matter. The date never came to pass.

Sister Anna and I kept in touch until her death. She remained a notable influence throughout my life, often offering guidance and advice, both solicited and unsolicited.

You Know What, Sister?

My freshman year meant sitting through a mandatory sex-ed class taught by Sr. Georgiana. Not only did she teach us the "the birds and the bees" but anatomy, too. It was amazing how much Sister knew about sex. Curiosity got the best of me. I raised my hand and politely asked how she became so knowledgeable. Sister shot me a stern look and, in all seriousness, said, "I wasn't always a nun, you know!" The entire class sucked in air and then let out a collective gasp when her words sank in. From that day forward we paid close attention to everything Sr. Georgiana had to say.

Socks-Off Sock Hop

The Carmelite nuns at my high school wouldn't allow us to take off our socks at the sock hops because "you could never tell what might come off next." We really couldn't dance very well because we slid all over the gym floor.

Avoiding Sin: Avoiding Private Parts

Now, Where Exactly Are Those?

On the issue of private parts, I was completely lost throughout Sr. Faustina's daily diatribes on the topic. I remember in the second grade her telling us, "Touching your private parts is like breaking down a fence and going onto someone's land and destroying their house."

Later that night during my bath, and thinking about Sister's words, I searched all over my body for those dotted lines. I still didn't know where those broken fences were! Finally, the next day I asked a girl sitting next to me where to find our private parts. Somewhat embarrassed, she pointed me in the right direction.

Bye-Bye Birdie

As I sat in the pew at weekly Mass, I crossed my legs and gently swung one of my legs back and forth. In a flash, Sister Blandina was at my side whispering a warning in my ear, "The good angel flew off and the devil flew on, and he was chanting: 'Swing me, swing me, swing me, you're giving me a free ride.'"

I had no idea what she was talking about but I shared her words with my mother when she picked me up from school. With a strange look on her face and curlers in her hair (very popular in the '70s), my mother flew to the school like a bat out of hell where she told Sr. Blandina she wouldn't let her ruin my life. What was that all about? I was only a second grader and didn't understand the confrontation.

It wasn't until many years later when I was earning my master's degree in education and studying early childhood behavior I realized Sr. Blandina must have thought I was masturbating! Really, I swung my legs out of boredom.

Little Boys Grow Up

A dear friend of mine, Louise, was bathing her infant son when her visiting aunt, a nun, checked in on her. Sister Dominic grew up in a family with only girls and she admitted to Louise she never before had seen a naked male. Intrigued, she watched Louise's every move. As Louise washed and powdered her son, Sr. Dominic couldn't stop staring at his "manhood." Finally, she turned her eyes away and asked, "Does 'it' get any larger? It seems very small."

Safety-Pin Snafu

A group of us eighth-grade girls were sitting at the lunch table when Claire's bra strap broke. Claire was well endowed, with breasts the size of watermelons. When the strap broke, one of the watermelons fell out, right on her lap.

I was the only one at the table with a safety pin, so I went with Claire to the bathroom to help her repair the damage. Once in the bathroom, I helped unzip her uniform and had my hand inside her dress. I was helping her pin the strap back together again when Sr. Sebastian stormed through the door.

"We finally got you, Miss Wilson. We send our trash to the public schools." She reported me to the prefect of discipline, who wouldn't believe that I was only pinning her strap. I had no idea what they thought I might have been doing. She ordered me to spend the rest of the semester leaning against a wall for "contaminating" the other girls.

Later that evening, my boyfriend explained to me that the nuns must have thought I was a lesbian trying to "take advantage" of Claire's big bosom. I didn't even know what a lesbian was! I really was just trying to help fix her strap.

Avoiding Sin: Avoiding the Opposite Sex

Ya Gotta Impress the Girls
Sitting behind Max, I thought of a way to get even with him for teasing me earlier in the day. His jacket was slung over the back of his chair, so I got back at him by tying his sleeve into a knot. After the dismissal bell rang, Max snatched his jacket off the back of the chair and jabbed his arm through the sleeve—completely ripping off the sleeve! That night Sr. Mary Joseph telephoned Max's mother and told her he was trying to show off for the girls by tearing off his clothes.

Me and My Shadow, Er, Spirit
Whenever Sister Ruth saw a boy and girl standing too close to each other, she would tell them, "There's no room for the Holy Spirit."

Dancing Partners
Sister Therese advised us girls to not dance with each other. It looked queer, she would say. Of course, she meant "strange." Little did she know!

Golden Boy
While walking home from high school in 1967, my best friend and I stumbled across a case of Man Tan shaving lotion thrown out on the street for garbage pickup. Man Tan was supposed to combine scented shaving lotion with a tanning agent to give your face a healthy, gold-bronzed look. Why would anyone throw that away?

This had to be really great stuff. If it could tan our faces, why not slather it all over our bodies so we could be sun gods like the Beach Boys?

That night we covered ourselves in the tanning lotion, only to discover that instead getting a healthy golden look and an alluring fragrance, we ended up heavily perfumed and our skin casting an unnatural orange glow. We looked like two young University of Texas Longhorn fans painted for the big game and stinking like the inside of a French whorehouse.

Not at all happy with the results, we tried to wash off the lotion. It wouldn't come off! It seems Man Tan was designed to indelibly stain your skin so you didn't have to keep applying it. We frantically continued to scrub off the orange stain, right up to the moment we had to go to class and face Sister Perpetua. A tough-as-nails South Chicago Felician nun, Sister Perpetua enjoyed spending her spare time reading the story of *Brass Knucks Nick* to the class. We tried to hide behind our classmates but Sister caught sight of the orange glow and directed us to the front of the room.

"Well, well, well, boys, what have you done to yourselves?" she sneered, enjoying equally our squirms of embarrassment and the snickers of our classmates. After hearing our story, she said, "Since you're already a distraction to the class, you might as well go ahead and really stick out." She ordered us to stand by our seats the entire morning.

We got a few laughs and comments of pity from the girls but it still wasn't worth it. Except for the golden memories, that is.

Let Me Hold That Ladder

The nuns at St. Clare all-girl high school finally relented and agreed to host a dance for their students and us, the boys at Mount St. Clare.

Since I was a responsible, helpful young man back in 1960, I volunteered to serve on the decorating committee. This move also meant spending the afternoon side by side with some of the young ladies at St. Clare trimming the auditorium. Unfortunately, I never made it to the dance that evening.

One of the girls and I decided to hang a few streamers from the ceiling. Since the only ladder available was a rickety wooden contraption that Paul Revere probably used to hang the lamp in the window of the old North Church, I gallantly offered to hold it while the girl hung the streamers.

As I steadied the ladder, I looked upward to make sure the girl was okay. Honest! Along came Mother John Neuman, who, summoning a force born from moral outrage backed by a solid 250 pounds, walloped me in the back of my head. She accused me of looking up the girl's skirt.

From that day forward, I was banished from all interschool activities. I was framed!

Avoiding Sin: Keeping Bodies Chaste, Clean, and Covered

Such a Tease!
Most of the nuns who taught me were pleasant. One math teacher, however, struck fear in our hearts. Her biggest pet peeve was girls teasing their hair into puffy bouffants. She even dragged one big-haired girl to the drinking fountain, dunked the girl's head under a stream of water, and successfully flattened her hair. Once when I was having a particularly flat and straight hair day because I was caught in the rain, Sister complimented me on my lovely hairdo. She even pointed out my soppy mess to the rest of the class. How embarrassing!

Seeing Red
My French teacher, Sr. Ruth, reached across in front of me in the classroom to dip her hand into the holy water font. I was standing so close that the sleeve of her habit brushed against my face. At our school, we were allowed to wear lipstick and I did—fire engine red. It smeared all over her habit. Sister used French that even a third-year French student couldn't understand.

Stolen Innocence
Toward the end of our fifth-grade year, most of us girls were well on our way toward puberty and pretty much knew the facts of life. One

of my classmates, Betty, was clueless, though. She had no idea where babies came from or why we were starting to shave our legs. The rest of us girls felt it our duty to inform her.

At recess we met behind the church barbecue pit with our "getting-to-know-your-body" books—the ones with the chickens in the first section and the mom and dad in the last part. We were just getting into the facts when we heard heavy breathing. Sister Mary Michael was standing behind us, her face redder than we had ever seen it before.

Sister marched all ten of us to the office and called all of our parents to come to school, including Betty's. Her mom and dad were hysterical, screaming how "those horrible little devils" (the other nine of us) had stolen their daughter's innocence.

Sister Mary Michael calmly looked Betty's mom square in the eyes and said in a low voice she thought we couldn't hear, "No, they were teaching her how *not* to have her innocence stolen."

Betty still had to stay away from the rest of us and we were forced to clean the parish grounds every afternoon for two weeks.

Prom-Dress Inspection

The morning of our high-school prom at our all-girl school, Sister Patricia required us girls to bring our dresses and shoes in for her inspection. She was clear on the shoes—no patent leather or any reflective material because they might show what was under our dress.

According to Sister's rules, we also were not allowed to wear dresses that revealed cleavage, or were in any way "suggestive." My sleeveless dress didn't pass muster that year. I added petite cap sleeves to finally gain her approval. If I hadn't, I wouldn't have been allowed into the dance.

Exposing Hem

On my first day in the fifth grade, Sr. Mary Bernadette required us girls to stand in front of the classroom so she could inspect the length of our skirts. She pulled us out of the line, one by one. Sister sent home instructions to our mothers to let out our hems so the skirts fell below the knees by at least an inch.

My mother, also a Catholic-school alumna, dutifully lengthened my skirt. I spent the entire fall of 1969 tripping over my uniform in the playground.

Cooler weather arrived and with it came a new coat—a fashionable, knee-length, plaid beauty with a matching red muff hat. There wasn't a day between Thanksgiving and early January that I didn't wear my beloved ensemble.

Naturally, with constant wear the coat grew dirty. While it was being dry-cleaned, I wore my old lime green coat from the previous year. So sixties-ish! Of course, I had grown a bit in the year, so my coat hung about three inches above the hem of my uniform. Well, not wanting to look like a dufus with my plaid skirt hanging below the lime jacket, I hiked up my skirt so it wouldn't show.

In a flash, Sister Mary Bernadette grabbed my ponytail and dragged me to the front of the classroom so she could inspect my hem. To my mortification, and right in front of my classmates, she yanked up my skirt, nearly exposing my panties. She chastised me for having "a hem so big and a skirt so short." I will never forget that embarrassment.

Hem Check—Busted!

Our principal was a stickler that we girls wear our uniforms with the proper hemline located just below the knees. We were heading back to our classrooms from first Friday Mass when Sister Irmingard called for a hem check. The girls ahead of me managed to slip by her and I also tried to scoot past her watchful eye because I had recently shortened my skirt to an unacceptable length. Of course, I was the one caught in her sting!

Sister Irmingard knelt on the floor, scissors in hand, and ripped out my skirt's hem in front of all the other students. I was so humiliated that for the remainder of my senior year I never shortened the skirt. Sister Irmingard has passed on, but I remember her fondly, despite the uncomfortable memories.

Clean Ears and Good Intentions

Our nuns insisted we practice good hygiene. They called for inspections, checking that our nails were clean and our ears wax-free. I had a crush on Patty, the most popular girl in second grade, but I knew she was headed for trouble. I noticed how waxy her ears were and I knew the nuns would give her a hard time. So I did what any red-blooded guy in love with a girl would do: I told her to clean her ears. The only problem was, I spoke too loudly.

Sister Helen heard me, and grabbing me by my ears, yelled, "Look at your own ears before you talk about those of others. You have the biggest, ugliest, elephant ears! Go fly away with your Dumbo ears and leave Patty alone!"

Swingset Panties

My cousins, who lived cross the street from me, attended the Catholic school while I went to the local public school. Afternoons and weekends were spent together, often playing in my yard.

Their nuns believed that girls should always wear skirts, even during playtime. They strongly encouraged girls to not wear shorts. Too unladylike, they claimed. My cousins wore gathered skirts created especially for playtime.

Playtime was a scene of irony and quite amusing for me. My cousins, in their skirts, always had their panties exposed. We "unladylike" girls, wearing shorts, kept ours hidden.

Paper Stockings

My friend Edna remembered as a youngster in Catholic school during the 1930s that she undertook an act of defiance by wearing ankle socks to classes instead of regulation knee socks.

As soon as Edna walked into the classroom, Sr. Martha nabbed her with one hand and grabbed sheets of paper off her desk with the other hand. Shoving the papers in Edna's hands, Sister instructed her to wrap them around her bare legs and to secure them with tape. Edna complied. She wore her new socks the entire day.

Leg Inspections

Our dress code required that we girls cover our legs with either stockings or anklets. When Sister Dolores was unsure whether or not a girl was wearing stockings, she ran her hand up and down the girl's legs.

———

Nuns' habits originally were designed to match women's wear of the day so that they could blend in with the communities they served. Someone lost sight of that by the 1960s. I don't recall any of my nuns wearing miniskirts and go-go boots. Maybe if they had, sisters wouldn't have been such an enigma to us.

Most of us wondered what they wore under their habits, if they ate dinner, or if they watched *Bonanza* on Sunday nights. Some of my friends took it a step further, badgering the nuns to invite them into the convent. My own sister even asked one of the nuns if she used soap!

I don't understand this curiosity. I didn't care if the sisters had hair or shaved their heads and the last thing I wanted was to visit where they slept. It was obvious from the way sisters chased us down and popped our hands with a pointer that they had legs and arms. Anything beyond that, I didn't want to know.

D. S.

Chapter Five

Shrouds of Mystery

"LOOK, I'M FLYING LIKE THAT TV NUN," Stephanie squealed, leaping from the jungle gym with one arm outstretched and the other holding a cardboard cornet in place on her head. "Don't you just wish our sisters wore habits that made them fly?"

"Oh, I'd like to see a few sisters take a flyin' leap, especially Sr. Boniface," Billy said, flipping a rock into the air. "And she can take all those rulers she shoves up her sleeves with her."

"I wonder how *do* they stick stuff up their sleeves and nothing ever falls out," Stephanie said. "Sister Ann Marie crams weird things up her sleeves, like dirty tissues, rosary beads—even my jacks and ball."

"Beats me. Maybe they've got secret pockets? Yeah, maybe they're really spies with secret mirrors in the backs of their veils and telephones in their shoes!"

"I know what they *don't* have under those habits," Stephanie teased, looking around to make sure no one could hear her.

"Hair."

"Ya mean they're bald? Oooh, yechhh!"

Playground banter shifted once again to familiar terrain—nuns' peculiar habits. Cloaked head-to-toe in black shrouds and living an austere lifestyle behind locked convent doors, nuns were an enigma to the world around them. An air of secrecy enveloped nuns.

A divine mystery.

The sixty-four-million-dollar question: who exactly were these women?

Much of the mystery centered on their habits, those they wore and the quirky ones they bore. Their signature garb—long, flowing gowns, veil and coif, thick stockings and clunky lace-up shoes—served as an unending source for burning questions. Did they have hair? Did they move by legs or were those wheels under their dresses? What did they wear underneath? What happened to those hankies and other items stuck up their sleeves?

Some of those questions found answers when a strong gust of wind blew or when Sister needed to scratch her head. For a lucky few, chance encounters provided explanations.

A young mother strolling with her daughter down the streets ran into one of her former nuns from St. Mary's. "Sister Timothy waved hello and then stuck her hand up her sleeve, fishing around as if she were trying to find something," Claire Hayward recalled more than sixty years later. The nun pulled a wrapped piece of licorice from out of her sleeve and handed it to the little girl.

"You keep *candy* in your habit?" the mother blurted.

An accidental sighting of a wisp of hair could send a flurry of whispers throughout a classroom but a total unveiling left kids thunderstruck. In once instance, softball-loving Sister Mary Carol jumped into a ballgame and threw off her headdress, sending a cascade of long blonde hair spilling down her back while her students watched in silent awe.

"All the kids loved Sr. Mary Carol. She was young, beautiful, and petite," Gina (Zucchero) Stamper recalled. "Especially the boys.

"Sister ignored all our stares. She simply rolled up her sleeves and grabbed a bat. Her beauty and spunk amazed us girls. I think it nearly killed the boys."

Catching a glimpse of a habit-less nun could be traumatic. When one young boy came home from school to find a room full of nuns milling around in gaily colored swimsuits (his mother was their seamstress), he begged his parents to transfer him to a nearby all-boy school taught by priests.

Karen Michaels remembers sneaking with a friend to the nuns' quarters at her all-girl boarding school in the late 1950s. Unlike the other boarders, Michaels lived year-round at the academy because she was an orphan. Michaels knew the lay of the land, even where the sisters swam.

"We hid in bushes near the pool hoping to catch a peek and not get caught," she said. Michaels admits to disappointment, at least initially. There was no fancy diving or even synchronized movements in the water, just swimming women wearing one-piece black swimsuits identical to those the girls wore.

"We soon realized not all the nuns wore black suits—some were nude!" Several sisters swam au natural, a sight Michaels still can't erase from her memory.

"I'm not exactly sure what we expected to find, but it certainly wasn't naked nuns."

Some children purposely searched out answers, often journeying to uncharted territory—the convent. Many walked in as guests but a few intrepid souls sneaked in. Two Starfleet officers-in-the-making at St. James Catholic School trekked uninvited through the convent, boldly going where no one had ever gone before. Not knowing (or caring) if they would face combatant Klingons or cuddly Tribbles, the young commandos actually *rifled* through nuns' personal items.

Paul Deran and his sixth-grade buddy were there because they earned the privilege of delivering daily mail to the convent. The youngsters did what any other red-blooded Catholic schoolchildren would do when given the opportunity: they nosed around.

"The first thing we did was read who the letters were addressed to and from where they were coming. We figured out the nuns' *real* names. Sister Immaculatta was Abby Foster and Sr. Catherine Elizabeth was Margaret Buckley," Deran recalled.

Mail delivery took them up and down convent hallways where they saw sisters' bras, panties, and slips—big ones—hanging from clotheslines. The boys couldn't wait to run back and report their findings. Unfortunately, their classmates didn't believe them.

"'Nuns don't wear bras and panties,' our friends insisted. 'Why would they? They're nuns,'" Deran said.

The general public regarded nuns as living holy cards, spiritual beings centered solely on prayer and leading children to God. Even adults who "knew better" couldn't help but fall into the trap of thinking nuns weren't fully human.

Wrong, wrong, wrong. Virginia Satir, the founder of an organization that trains people "to be more fully human" described living humanely as "a person who is real and is willing to take risks, to be creative, to manifest competence." Satir may not have realized it, but she described nuns.

Many sisters were athletic and sports-loving while others were keenly humorous, not above pulling a practical joke or two. Talents and interests varied from nun to nun, including some as unusual as those of Sister Steve, a cloistered nun who served her order as a finger-tapping ham-radio operator.

Habits and convent walls sheltered nuns from worldly influences. Many sisters led their lives under the belief that God provided for all their needs. That simple trust kept worries at bay, often gifting nuns with serenity during times of trial. One nun, formerly cloistered, was given charge of her order's postulants. She escorted the girls on an outing to the city and it was time to eat.

"I remembered a great deli from my days before the convent, so I took the girls there," she said. "'Eat up,' I told them. They were young girls and hungry." While they were eating, the Sister looked around the room and spotted a menu on the wall—with prices. Sister had forgotten she would need to pay for the meals! She opened her purse and found a few coins.

"I let the girls eat. God would take care of us," she recalled. Shortly before the girls finished, a woman who had sought Sister's counseling in the past walked into the deli.

"She was so excited to see me outside the convent that she insisted paying for all of our lunches."

Other times, nuns took advantage of the influence they held, especially when fully habited. Even though nuns were allowed to wear street clothing following Vatican II, one sister kept a traditional habit hanging in her closet to wear whenever she ventured into New York City.

"Sister said when she wore her habit, she 'made out better.' More people gave up their seats, opened her doors, and hailed taxis for her when she dressed traditionally," Dorothy Lister recalled.

Church reforms called for a sweeping change in nuns' lives, including urging them to update their habits. Finally, one of the Church's divine mysteries had been revealed, leading to money changing hands as children won and lost bets over whether or not the nuns really had arms, legs, and hair. At many parishes, children were given little advance warning about impending habit changes while in other parishes the introduction was announced months ahead, creating an aura of anticipation much like the arrival of the Beatles or the launch of the Mercury astronauts.

At St. Luke's in South Florida, Catholic children and their parents lined convent walkways and school halls as sisters wearing new digs paraded toward classrooms. Red-faced Sisters of Mercy passed through a gauntlet of onlookers in normal nun fashion: looking straight ahead and walking in step with each other. However, the nuns fidgeted, running their hands through their hair or tugging at their skirts. The new habits were created with the hot Florida sun in mind, and gone were traditional billowing sleeves. The sisters couldn't find a spot to shove their arms and hands.

Gradually, some nuns shed their habits entirely and allowed a necklace with a cross and a tiny pin designating their order, along with sensible shoes, as the remaining telltale signs to their identities. Catholics lived through "near-nun" experiences, leaving them bewildered and confused from trying to figure out "is she or isn't she?"

A few years after she left Catholic grade school, and the memories of one tough nun in particular, a teenage girl dining at a local restaurant thought her waitress looked familiar. She couldn't quite place her. Dawning came with a terrible shock—the waitress was Sister Thomas.

"Sister Thomas taught us in a straightforward, no-nonsense manner," Sheila Rooney recalled. "She taught us math timetables through songs, drilling us at least 500 times a day. She tapped rhythm with her pointer and kept us in line by reminding us how terrible we sounded, as if we were 'dragging garbage down Westfield Road,'" Rooney said.

"I didn't know a nun could abandon her vows," Rooney said years later, adding she worried for the nun's future because she had left her order. "I was shocked but I wondered if she was allowed to do that."

Nuns' appearance, age, and curious behavior contributed heavily to their mystique. Numerous former students remember nuns as being "nearly a hundred" years old when in fact the women most likely were in their thirties or forties. One man remembers a nun teaching him during the mid-1960s who had been a survivor of the sinking *Titanic* in 1912. In all fairness, he conceded, she might have been an infant or child when the ship sank, which meant the nun probably was in her fifties or sixties when she taught him.

Nuns' social interaction and relationships with people "on the outside" illustrated how the public perceived them differently from the way they actually were. A gruff, don't-bother-me sister revealed her gentle side to a parishioner in charge of painting convent walls.

"A new, hip pastor joined our parish in the 1960s," said Lynn Olivo. "He changed a number of items in our dress code, making life a lot more fun for us high-school students."

Father introduced a few changes to the nuns, too. At that time, nuns were allowed to have only white walls in their rooms. Father told them they could change the color to any pastel they desired.

"My father did all the painting for the church, including the convent," Olivo said. "Most of the sisters were thrilled and selected shades of light blue, green, yellow, and pink for Dad to paint."

One elderly nun, Sister Constance, couldn't be bothered with the fuss and told Olivo's dad she didn't "care for all this foolishness and paint it as you like."

He painted the room lavender. Sister Constance never said a word to my father but a few weeks later he received a gift, Olivo said. With it came a thank-you note signed "Miss Purple."

Some divine mysteries may never be explained or understood, but one mind-boggler nagging at more young Catholic minds than any other has been resolved: yes, they *do* have hair.

Habit Memories

Beneath the Habit: Appearances Matter

Gestapo Shoes

Our sisters wore black and bulky square-toed shoes with tie-up laces, like boots. Gestapo shoes. The steady *click, click, click* from sisters' shoes as they paced up and down our wooden-floored hallways filled me with terror. At first the clicking was faint, similar to the clatter of a dropped pencil. But with each passing moment, the clicking grew louder and louder until it reached a point that seemed deafening. Nuns were in pursuit! Silence replaced the clicking, signaling the end of the hunt. The sisters had tracked their prey. At that point, that's all I could do—pray.

Pink Nightgowns

Sister Barbara asked me to walk her to the convent and carry her briefcase. Once there, she asked if I wanted a tour. Sure thing, I said. Who would miss that opportunity?

She guided me down a hallway and pointed out each of the nuns' rooms, including hers. One of the other nuns called Sr. Barbara's name, so she stepped out of her room for a moment. As soon as she left, I opened her closet door, hoping to sneak a peek at God-knows-what. I wasn't disappointed! Hanging in front of me was a nightgown as pink as a Florida flamingo.

I was dumbfounded. I thought nuns wore black—black everything! I figured something must have been a little off with Sister Barbara for her to wear pink.

Volkswagen-Bug Nuns

My sister and I were driving down the highway behind a Volkswagen Beetle sometime back in the 1960s, not long after that car company had introduced headrests—one of the first manufacturers to do so.

"Look at those nuns in that car ahead of us," my sister said. "We've been traveling behind them for several miles and neither one of them has turned her head.

"They just keep staring straight ahead. Isn't that strange?"

I took a good look at the nuns ahead of us and then burst into laughter when I realized why the nuns' heads weren't turning. Apparently, my sister mistook the new-fangled headrests for the oversized headdress worn by some orders of nuns.

Get Thee to a Nunnery, er, Boys' School?

My mother helped the nuns by hemming and sewing clothes for them. The sisters wore habits covering them from head to toe and weren't allowed to wear street clothes as they do today, so most of mother's seamstress work involved sewing undergarments and mending their habits.

The sisters occasionally swam at a nearby pool, so my mother's project one spring day was sewing new bathing suits for them. The suits were modest and one-piece, but jazzy, too, made from fabrics in bright, shimmering colors with patterns and flowers.

One afternoon, several nuns had come to our house for a fitting. My brother Pete bounded in from school, rushing in to say hello only to catch sight of the sisters milling around our living room looking like Esther Williams understudies. Shocked, he turned around and left without saying a word.

Later that night, he dropped a bombshell on my parents. He told them he wanted to leave St. Anthony's and attend St. Bruno's, an all-boy school nearby.

"It's wrong for nuns to wear bathing suits and swim in public," he said. "I can't look at the sisters again and not think of them disgracing themselves."

Whatever holy ideals Pete held about the nuns were shattered when he realized the sisters were just "regular" people like us.

Medieval to Modern

I attended St. Mark's in the mid-1960s when the Church introduced its reforms. For my first two years there, our nuns wore floor-length habits with waist-length veils.

During the middle of my second year, Sister Mary Phillip entered class wearing a knee-length habit and a short veil with a clump of blonde hair peeking out. My jaw dropped! I thought nuns were bald.

The next year we moved and I attended St. William of York. The nuns there didn't even wear habits. The only way we could tell the nuns apart from the laity were by crosses worn around their necks. In one year's time, the nuns transformed from medieval to modern, at least in their manner of clothing.

The Unveiling

Our principal, Sister Monica, announced over the public address system that the following day our sisters would be dressed a little differently. She warned us not to make any comments.

What in the heck was she talking about? I stared at Sister Priscilla, my second-grade teacher. Sweet and young, Sister gracefully cruised up and down the aisles, her ankle-length dress billowing around her and her veil flapping slightly as she bent over a child's work.

The following day, I arrived at school to find Sister Priscilla standing in front of the classroom wearing a just-below-the knee white dress, nude stockings, simple black shoes, a short black veil and...hair! Sister had hair! That was so cool. We kids assumed nuns shaved their heads.

No Nun Later...What a Shock

The striking woman sipping her cocktail at the bar looked familiar. She was a few years older than the rest of us so she couldn't have been one of my classmates attending our grade-school reunion.

I studied the woman, trying to place her. Attractive and stylish, the woman laughed affably as she shot the breeze with a few of my buddies. Finally, I introduced myself to her.

"You don't remember me, do you?"

Now I was stumped.

"I was one of your teachers at St. Pious."

One of my teachers? A nun! Or was she?

Sitting before me was my eighth-grade teacher—my favorite. Instead of a habit and clunky black shoes, Sister Hilary wore a classy tailored dress and high heels. And she was drinking a highball!

"How could you do this to me? It's just not right," I managed to tell her, still astonished. This took place at that time when the Church went through its revolution. I think they called it Vatican II. It just wasn't right.

Hey, Good Lookin'

Sister Thomas Aquinas taught us needlework, among other things, and looked as though butter wouldn't melt in her mouth. One day, she vanished from our school. We soon heard she'd been spotted on Twickenham Broadway wearing a miniskirt and fishnet stockings. No one at school ever mentioned her again.

Beneath the Habit: Sisters Say and Do the Darndest Things

Do Nuns Have Periods?

Alice and I were busy cleaning the convent, our weekly chore, when a strange thought struck us: do nuns have menstrual periods?

We had just finished listening to "the talk," and the concept of a nun undergoing the same monthly mystery held us in rapt discussion for more than twenty minutes as we dusted and vacuumed the sisters' living quarters. Our talk didn't resolve our questions, so we poked around while we cleaned.

Alice and I rummaged through closets, opened drawers, and peeked into medicine cabinets in a hunt to discover even just one tampon or sanitary napkin. We searched in fear, worried that one of those old creaks and moans coming from the wooden floorboards would be a nun catching us in the act of what surely must have been a mortal sin! The hunt continued, even though we never discovered proof nuns had periods.

We decided maybe God blessed nuns so they wouldn't have periods like the rest of us women.

Want Fries with That?

My mother drove a group of young sisters from San Diego to Los Angeles for investure as postulates and novices into their order, Sisters of St. Joseph of Corondolet. This took place on a Friday when we observed rules of fasting and abstinence, which included not eating meat. The Archbishop gave all present at the ceremony a dispensation from the rules. On the way home, my mother pulled into a drive-in restaurant and the carhop took our orders.

My mother and I ordered fish while my sister and a couple of the nuns ordered eggs. Sister Patricia closed her menu and said to the carhop, "I'll take a hamburger and french fries, please." The carhop, clearly a good Catholic boy, nearly fainted.

"It's all right dear. Today is the Feast of St. Joseph and we are the Sisters of St. Joseph," Sister Patricia blubbered, trying to ease his mortification. I don't think he bought it.

That's a Big 10-4, Sister Buddy

I was listening to my amateur radio one Saturday morning when I received a strong Morse code signal at quite a respectable speed. As we say in ham-radio lingo, the operator had a "good fist," which meant the "ham" was extremely skilled. Morse code is highly technical and nearly a lost art. Finding an adept ham operator is a rarity.

The operator identified herself as Sister Steve, a member of a cloistered order. I was a bit surprised. I'm not Catholic, but my understanding of cloistered orders is that members couldn't communicate with outsiders.

Sister Steve said she "spreads the gospel" of ham radio to other convents, thus helping them save money on long-distance phone charges. To keep her ministry flowing, she was granted special permission to use her ham radio recreationally, communicating with the general public like me so her skills could remain sharp.

"But how in the world did you become interested in ham radio?" I tapped in code to her.

"A man selling me an arc welder introduced me to the hobby," she tapped back.

"For what possible reason would you, a nun, need an arc welder?"

"To fix the plumbing, of course."

I thought something was amiss in our transmission until Sister Steve explained since her order was cloistered, each of the nuns was assigned a secular duty to support the operation of the convent. Sister Steve was the maintenance "man."

Nun Un-Corked

Louise was a rambunctious teenager and spiraling out of control. Her aunt, Sister Dominic, suggested she stay at her convent for a weekend in order to "straighten her out."

When Louise arrived, a frail, elderly nun greeted her. The two visited for a bit when Sister took a bottle of sacramental wine out of a cabinet and handed it to Louise.

"Would you mind opening the bottle for me? My hands just aren't what they used to be," the nun said.

Louise did as she was asked and the nun promptly rewarded her with a glass of wine, the girl's first ever. Sister poured herself a glass and the two settled into an evening of drinking. They got tipsy.

After Sister Dominic chastised Louise for drinking, she told her the elderly nun asked Louise to open the wine bottle because the other nuns were well aware of Sister's tendency to indulge and always refused to open the bottle.

Next Thing, We'll Have Mud Wrestling

In the late '60s, I was the interim food service manager at an all-girl Catholic college. It was a quaint school, nestled on top of a rolling hillside. The college recently had relaxed restrictions on male visitation, so it became common to see boys and girls strolling across campus hand-in-hand. It was not unusual to even see a few boys kissing coeds good-bye when the girls retreated to their dorms.

One of the elderly nuns from school helped me out in the cafeteria from time to time, scrubbing pots and pans. She never had much to say. She just slipped into the kitchen, scouring her pots and pans, and left.

Soon after the ban on boys was lifted, Sister stormed into the kitchen, mumbling to herself. She grabbed the pots and thrashed them about, almost violently.

I was concerned she might be having a heart attack or experiencing some other health problem, so I approached her work area to investigate. She was slinging pots and wailing, "Boys kissing the girls, girls holding boys' hands, young people hugging in the sanctuary. This college is nothing more than a whorehouse on top of a hill."

I couldn't believe my ears!

They Need What?

My dad owned a pharmacy in a small Pennsylvania town where he dispensed medicines and distributed hygiene products to the nuns and priests. I was helping him out one day when I noticed he had placed Modess sanitary pads in with the rest of the sisters' order.

Why in the world did Dad do that, I wondered? Why would nuns need sanitary napkins? For all we thought, nuns didn't even have breasts under those bulky habits, much less any other feminine trappings.

Bonfire Madness

Bill, a CPA, had been spending his weekdays auditing the books of one of his favorite clients, the local order of nuns. He was assisted by Sister Gloria, a sweet, elderly nun who served as the order's bookkeeper.

He had been reviewing various receipts from a few years earlier related to the sale of their convent and school when he discovered a tax-deduction letter referring to an antique chair valued at $1,000. He pointed that item out to Sister Gloria and to Mother Superior Berthold, who had popped in to see how the audit was moving along.

"Oh, my heavens," said a dazed mother superior. "We had dozens of those chairs throughout the convent! What happened to them, Sr. Gloria?"

Sister Gloria, squirming in her chair, hemmed and hawed but finally answered.

"Do you remember how excited we were when we finally sold the convent," Sister asked. "And we built a blazing bonfire to celebrate?"

"A few of us sisters were caught up in keeping the flames stoked so we tossed anything in the fire we could find. Someone remembered the old chairs and, well...."

Silence filled the room.

"We'll just keep that bit of information among ourselves," Mother Superior said.

Cecelia in the Convent

I was only twelve years old when my older sister joined a cloistered order. When Cecelia first entered the convent, we only could visit by speaking with her through bars in the foyer. She wasn't allowed to come home and visit us, not even to attend my brother's funeral when he was killed in World War II. Eventually, the order dropped its rules of cloister and my sister ventured out into the world. She learned to speak nine languages and became a linguist for her order. Cecelia has been in the order for nearly sixty years and has been nothing but happy in the convent.

Nuns of the Wild West

I visited an art collective housed in a building well over 150 years old on the San Antonio Riverwalk in Texas. Originally, it was the site of a convent and girls' school run by Ursuline nuns. I had attended a high school taught by nuns in that order, so I was immediately drawn to the site.

Of particular interest in the building was a trap door hidden in the floor. As the story goes, Comanche Indians periodically raided the town, looking for ammunition and God knows what else. The Ursulines gathered the girls in their charge and spirited them to the trap door. The door was an entryway to an underground tunnel leading to the San Antonio River where the girls hid until all was clear. The sisters then trooped the young girls back to the convent.

Musical Chairs

My aunt, Sister Winifred, or Sister Winnie as everyone called her, was a frequent dinner guest in our home. During one visit, my dad invited his driver, an elderly Italian man, to eat with us. When we approached the dinner table, Mr. Delvici pulled out a chair for Sister Winnie.

Looking a bit confused, Sister Winnie stepped away from the chair and started to sit in the one next to it. Again, Mr. Delvici pulled that chair out from the table.

"Oh, you can sit in that chair if you like, I'll choose another," a baffled Sister told Mr. Delvici as she moved toward another chair.

"No, Sister, this chair is for *you*," Mr. Delvici said. "This is my act of courtesy and respect."

"Oh! I guess no one has ever done that for me before."

Doggone It!

The nuns at my children's school gave us a dog. We went out for the day, leaving the doggie alone. When we returned, we found our home torn apart. The drapes were chewed and torn and the sofa ripped.

Not long after that, I was visiting with our pastor, Monsignor Ray, and mentioned what the sisters' destructive dog did to our house. "Hmm, no wonder I had to buy so many habits for them," Monsignor replied.

Sister Sleds
On Saturday my buddies and I were sledding down the hill where our school was located. A nun stepped out of the convent and asked to borrow a sled. None of us had ever seen a sister sledding, so we were game and handed her one. We were amazed to see Sister gliding down the hill. What a story to share at school the following week. I mentioned Sister's hillside escapade to my homeroom nun, who then told me many of the sisters ventured out late at night and sledded down the hill. We never knew for sure if they actually conducted nightly runs down the hill but figured they probably did since we all knew nuns didn't lie.

Holy Rollers
One Saturday morning a group of us met at the school gymnasium to shoot hoops. We thought we had the entire gym to ourselves until we walked downstairs to use the bathroom, where we heard music floating from a nearby room. The doors were locked but we could peek through a crack in the double doors leading to the music. Several nuns were roller skating!

Um, Yummy Pie
My mom and aunt were helping out in the kitchen at a school chili supper, alongside our principal, Sr. Mary Leo. The women were cutting up desserts and placing them on paper plates when my mom noticed how sloppy a chocolate meringue pie looked.

"Oh, this thing is a mess," my mom said. "We can't possibly put that on the buffet table!"

"You're right," my aunt agreed. "The woman who prepared this must not have much in the way of culinary skills. Who do you suppose baked it?"

Later that evening my mom and aunt discovered who the chef was—Sr. Mary Leo! To their mortification, she had heard every word they said.

Stuffed Love

One of my fondest memories was the year our Parent/Teacher Organization decided to purchase the nuns Christmas gifts more to their liking, rather than for practicality. The good sisters requested stuffed animals. As president of the PTO, my father helped deliver the gifts to them on Christmas Day. He never before had seen such a delightful reaction from the sisters, he told us later that day. The nuns acted as if they were kids again, hugging the plush toys and laughing at each other. When I returned to class after the holidays, my homeroom nun could hardly wait to show us the green bunny Santa delivered.

Beneath the Habit: Unforgettable Presence

Look at Me, Class

Sister Fifi, as the older girls called her behind her back, was typical of most of the nuns at Blessed Sacrament. She was old. In fact, Sister Fifi was *very* old. She already had retired once. Because of a growing nun shortage in 1969, Church leaders pulled her out of mothballs to teach my sixth-grade class.

Sister Fifi had a face no one could forget. Right in the middle of her lower lip, directly in front of her teeth, a fleshy growth hung for all to see. The knob measured at least an inch long, according to my eleven-year-old imagination.

The daily grind grew too much for Sister Fifi. When she tired, which happened more frequently as the school year wore on, Sister noisily sucked the growth into her mouth and held it between her teeth until it was time to talk. Then, explosively, the growth shot out of her mouth as she spoke.

She captured our attention that year. All eyes remained focused on Sister Fifi's mouth. This had become the most fascinating, yet most repulsive, spectacle of our young lives.

What Was That Odor?

One of the nuns who taught at our school passed away when I was in first grade. Of course, all students were required to attend her funeral Mass. I had never been to one before so I didn't know what to expect.

After school, I rushed into the house and blurted to my mother, "Dead nuns stink."

Mom stared at me for a few minutes. Then she laughed. She figured out I mistook the burning incense, traditionally lit at Catholic funerals, for the dear, departed nun's odor.

Sister Green Bay Packer
Of all the nuns at St. Rita, Sister Jude was the one you never wanted to anger. She wore a three-inch scar on her chin and resembled Green Bay Packer Jimmy Taylor after a rough day on the frozen tundra of Lambeau Field. She might have been as strong as him, too. Sister Jude's calm outward demeanor didn't fool us. We knew if she ever grabbed us by the neck, a clothesline tackle was coming next.

Nun Encounter
When I was a child, my mother brought me to visit a nun who practically raised my mom, who was an orphan. Sister must have been a hundred years old. Mom asked her how she was doing and the nun mentioned she was bothered by a little arthritis in her hand.

"I know how you got that," my mom said. "All those years clutching the ruler."

"Oh, you were always such a rascal," Sister chuckled.

Sister Goat Gruff
Our family would drive across the border to Zaragossa, Mexico, so we five boys could get haircuts and our parents could buy meat, baked goods, and non-perishable groceries. On our return trip, we often passed farms outside El Paso where we shopped at vegetable and fruit stands. At one of our stops we saw a sign that read, "Goats for Sale." My youngest brother begged dad to buy a goat. My father, somewhat impulsive, caved in and purchased it.

"We can have milk and make cheese," my dad rationalized to my mother when we arrived home with the smelly goat in tow.

Mother wasn't happy. We were a city family, she said, and had only our backyard in which to keep the animal. Besides, how do we expect to get milk from a male goat, she asked.

Checking the animal's sex never occurred to us. We chose the goat because its face resembled someone we all knew: Sister Magdalena.

Mom made us keep the "stinky" goat outside in the yard, but since goats are great jumpers and climbers, "Nanny" didn't stay there long. Over the fence and running loose in the neighborhood, the goat led the ten of us kids (children, not goats) and my father in a frantic chase up and down the block, over lawns and through gardens. After an hour of chasing him, we finally caught up with the goat and secured him in the backyard. In less than ten minutes the goat ate through the rope and made his way back over the fence. Once again, the chase was on!

The goat took a different route and headed down a strip of land between the school and convent where he came face-to-face with Sr. Magdalena. The two locked eyes. Sister pointed her finger straight at him, just as she had done to me many times. Nanny froze in his tracks. She kept her finger pointed in his direction as she inched closer. The goat stood still until Sr. Magdalena got close enough to grab its collar.

"You know, he looks a bit like my brother," Sister said, adding that her brother was deceased.

After the second escape, Mom put her foot down and ordered us to get rid of the goat. We tried giving Nanny to Sr. Magdalena but she explained the pastor wouldn't put up with the goat eating the church grass, hedges, and flowers.

"The goat has given me happy memories," Sister said when she came to say her good-byes to Nanny. "It has been a long time since I've thought so much about my brother."

We returned the goat to the farmer, sans refund. Everything happens for a reason. We got a goat, not for milk and cheese but for the chance of bringing a sister and brother back together again.

Angry Sister

One of the most important lessons I learned was not to anger Sister.

If you did, first thing you knew, Sister's face would be in your face. Her eyes turned into slits. Not good. Then her mouth twitched and twisted into an unfathomable distortion that had to be seen to be believed.

Those habit sleeves, the ones where anything could come flying out of, even a mile-long ruler, were rolled up to her elbows. Sister was ready to blow and our young bodies needed as much protection as possible. Our brains sent automatic signals to lift our hands over our heads. We did, with no awareness of memories of even raising our arms.

No matter what moves we made, Sister was always faster. After a "put your hands down, young lady," followed by a "put your hand out, missy," Sister fulfilled her duty, which she believed we always brought upon ourselves.

Nuns have been given a hard rap over discipline. Sure, they were strict. I remember getting whacked with a black rubber-tipped pointer a couple of times but I also recall instances the sisters let slide when I should have been disciplined. Some of the stunts I pulled would fall under zero tolerance today and boot me into detention, like the time I shot Carol in the eye with a spitwad. These days, if I had referred to Sister Mary Ann as "creep in front of the room" in a note tossed to a *boy* during prayers, the least I could expect would be a trip to the principal's office. If I had brought the book *Devils and Demons* into a Catholic classroom today the way I did forty years ago, I'd be signed up for therapy—or an exorcism. By modern standards, I may have had it easy with the sisters.

D. S.

Chapter Six

Knuckle Cracks and Group Slaps: Sisterly Tough Love

THE NUN AT ST. HELEN'S orphanage wasn't taking any guff from Jake and Elwood, even if they recently had been released from prison. She wasn't about to give them the go-ahead to steal money on her behalf. Nor was she going to let her two former students spew vulgarities—and call her a fat penguin, to boot.

Smack. Down came the ruler on Jake's hand. *Crack*, on Elwood's knuckles and then back to Jake and then to Elwood as each of them spat out a curse. Realizing her errant boys had not learned their lessons, the nun pulled out a sword and sent Jake and Elwood scrambling.

That hilarious scene from the *Blues Brothers* movie embodied common perception of sisterly law and order. Catholics and non-Catholics alike saw nuns as masters of discipline. With one silent wave of a stick, usually a twelve-inch ruler, nuns simultaneously produced terror and respect from their students.

Long stereotyped as ruler-wielding knuckle-crackers, Catholic nuns were much more resourceful disciplinarians than public perception suggested. They set rigid behavioral standards and relied upon a vast arsenal of creative weaponry to help students meet those standards.

Old-fashioned brute force was often the first armament a nun pulled out of her cache. From the beginning of time, God's holy warriors have been muscling out evil, relying on both inner and outer strength. Saint Michael the Archangel didn't exactly open the door to hell for Lucifer and suggest he live in a warmer climate. Drawing on fury, the Archangel *battled* Satan and his demons, bouncing them straight to eternity's furnace.

So why shouldn't a nun be allowed a bit of leeway?

A little nunly roughhousing left an indelible impression on students. Considering most sisters stood less than five feet tall and were approaching the century mark (according to forty-year-old recollections), the sight of a sister changing from meek Dr. Banner into a seething, vein-popping Hulk-in-a-veil left more than one child dumbstruck.

Sam Miller recalled that slightest infractions, including not knowing an answer to a question, transformed his eighth-grade teacher into Sr. Raging Bull. Once, she stormed down the aisle to Miller's desk where she grabbed him by his belt buckle, lifted him out of the chair, and dangled him as if he were a limp rag doll.

Unlike Dr. Banner, nuns didn't rely on gamma radiation to spark their metamorphism. Simply banging kneelers in church or forgetting to turn off the holy water tank spigot could send sparks flying. For Sr. John Paul, an off-the-cuff sexual wisecrack lit her keg of dynamite.

Matt, Camden Catholic High School's starting quarterback, was bragging in chemistry class about an athletic feat when Sr. John Paul tried lowering his ego a notch or two.

"You're still a babe in the woods, Matt," Sister teased.

"I'd like to have a babe in the woods," he muttered.

Turning on her heels, Sr. John Paul grabbed Matt by his collar, yanked him out of his desk, and lifted him off the ground. "Never *ever* talk like that in my class again," she said, tightening her grip and speaking slightly above a whisper.

"Matt was a big guy and Sister was not," according to his classmate, Patrick M. Arnold. "Sister left us speechless."

Often, nuns found the need to supplement force with artillery. Nun lore describes how they inflicted punishment with rulers, but the women actually relied on a variety of munitions. Just as any good military leader might evaluate a combat zone, sisters also made their own assessments and then called on support: pointers, chalkboard erasers, yardsticks, switches from trees, and even parts of their habits. One nun's injury actually led to the creation of a new discipline tool.

"Sister Peter Claver was a large, powerful woman who thought nothing of slapping you on the back if she liked you or slapping you silly if she did not. Luckily, she liked me," recalled Theresa Pulley. The nun slipped on ice one winter, breaking her arm and giving her students cause to celebrate a whack-less winter. No such luck, Pulley said. Sister Peter continued thumping students with her cast until the arm healed.

Although it appeared most nuns relied on whatever tool of destruction was handiest, one Midwest nun was particular—and resourceful. Once school let out for summer, Sr. James Michael visited farm implement dealers at her county's annual fair and collected promotional yardsticks. Some dealers even set aside cases for Sister's visit. Over the years farm dealers stopped giving away yardsticks, probably stemming from post-traumatic stress disorder suffered by John Deere or Massey Ferguson executives once taught by Sr. James Michael.

DISCIPLINE YOU WOULDN'T SEE IN TODAY'S PC CLASSROOM

- Sitting in a metal trash can in the corner of the classroom, facing classmates
- Pulling pigtails and ponytails
- Sticking gum in a child's own hair (when caught chewing in class)
- Placing a "detention hat"—an old fur cap—on a child's head and forcing him or her to wear it after school

---

Sisters were masters of the mind, often augmenting intimidation and fury with psychological terrorism. Borrowing from the Central Intelligence Agency's handbook on guerrilla warfare, many nuns recognized once they reached a child's mind there would be no need for corporal punishment. If Tokyo Rose had been as well practiced in mental manipulation as Catholic nuns, Kentucky Fried Sushi would be the leading fast-food chain in America today.

For Sr. Martin, creating shame and guilt in her students worked miracles in maintaining order and deterring misbehavior. She printed each of her sixty first graders' names on a grid on the blackboard in the back of the classroom. When children violated a class rule, Sister ordered them out of their seats and sent them on her version of the Bataan Death March to the back of the room. Once there, amidst disproving stares from their classmates, students placed a demerit next to their names. Offenders hung their heads in shame and trudged back to their desks.

"Early in the year, a boy sitting next to me asked me a question, which I answered," said Peggy (Carter) Wehe. "Sister Martin caught my part of the exchange and ordered me to the back of room. I was mortified!"

"I marched to the back of the room in shame. I couldn't bear the disapproving stares of 120 eyes. That was my first—and last—demerit of the school year," she said.

Many nuns relied on creating fear, especially of the unknown, and letting a child's own mind rein in his behavior. Mary Ellen Grabow credited Sr. Mary Phillip's "glue machine" for keeping her in line. As a chatty first grader, Grabow had difficulty not talking. At one point, exasperated by Grabow's inability to keep quiet, Sr. Mary Phillip held a small brown bottle containing clear glue and waved it for all to see.

"Do you see this bottle of glue?" she snapped. "This is Johnny Richards."

Everyone knew about Johnny. Rumors had it he attended the school some years back but mysteriously left without saying his good-byes. The children couldn't take their eyes off the bottle.

"Keep talking and you'll be the next victim in the glue machine," Sr. Mary Phillip warned.

Even though she quivered in terror from Sister's warnings, Grabow couldn't stop chitchatting.

"Sister took my hand and led me out the door and down the hallway toward the fourth-grade classroom where my meltdown awaited. As we entered the room, she flipped a switch on the wall that supposedly turned on the glue machine in a back room."

A thunderous clanging erupted from behind a back wall. It was true, Sister really did turn children into sticky goo, Grabow reminisced.

"I pitched a wailing fit, promising Sister I would be good and never talk again. I must have convinced her because she took my hand and led me, sobbing, down the hall to my classroom."

Grabow later discovered Sr. Mary Phillip turned on a light switch in a coat closet that signaled a couple of fourth graders to "warm up" the glue machine by pounding metal buckets with broom handles.

Catholics believe the Church is "one body," an all-for-one, one-for-all community of those living here on earth, in heaven with God, or in purgatory, heaven's waiting room. Many nuns doled out punishment using a similar three-Musketeer approach, incorporating peer pressure and urging children to snitch on each other.

Nuns routinely instructed children to rat on each other. Most children squealed away, recognizing in themselves a sense of honor and duty to do the right thing. That, and knowing if they didn't comply Sister would levy a harsher punishment on them.

In some instances, the sisters ferreted out offenders by threatening to take away special privileges such as class parties and field trips. To help students take her warnings seriously, Sister Bridget held a sixth-grade class hostage and treated them to her version of the Spanish Inquisition. She had a good reason. The teacher discovered a note with the words "do this" and a drawing of an obscene finger gesture in the student council suggestion box.

The nun kept the kids captive. No more recess, she ordered. No more talking during lunch and no more early dismissals on Saints' days (except for St. Patrick; Sr. Bridget was Irish). Other than an uneasy glance here and there, no one budged. They were comrades in crime. The perp's identity was safe—until Sr. Bridget threatened to take away a student trip to Washington D.C.

Loose lips might have sunk ships but in that schoolroom they were flapping away. Students couldn't get to lifeboats quick enough, and no one was stopping to help a classmate aboard. Chaos erupted and class calm degenerated into a *Lord of the Flies* rendition with brother turning against brother. The ship was sinking fast but the culprit never 'fessed up, despite accusations flying around the room.

While many nuns jumped through hoops to single out a misbehaving child, others didn't even bother, and instead, assigned group penance. Forms of atonement varied, from Sister calling everyone's parents to lining the children up and administering a group ruler-whack or face-smack. Ed Crann recounts a gang slap after several of the boys goofed off during Mass.

Sister lined up all the boys in the front of the room execution-style, sans blindfolds and final cigarettes. The students faced outward with their hands tucked behind them while Sister walked down the row and cuffed them one by one on the face.

"We face-slapped veterans took it all in stride. It was just another day at the office," Crann said. "In fact, it became sort of a macho contest to see who could laugh after getting whacked."

The rookies—the boys who never got in trouble—didn't fare as well, Crann said.

"It was an ugly scene seeing those boys bawl like babies or drop to the floor like soccer players on ESPN do when they're faking an injury. I know they didn't deserve it, but I admit enjoying watching some of them walk a mile in my PF Flyers for a change."

Some nuns resorted to name-calling, throwing out "cheeky" and "bold-and-brassy pea" to mouthy girls. Sister Beatrice kept taunts within a religious context, admonishing one third-grade boy with, "As it was in the beginning, is now and forever shall be, you're totally worthless!" At least the child had a heads-up on learning the Glory Be.

Maybe because they spent evenings glued to *Get Smart* and *The Jetsons*, or perhaps because they were overwhelmed with Cold War fears, some nuns bypassed rulers and pointers in favor of the latest high-tech gadgetry. A couple of nuns threatened to connect their students to lie detectors. One of them, Sr. Edmund, actually frightened her students into submission by telling them their parents would have to buy the lie detector. Just what every kid needed, a lie detector in the living room!

Not all discipline was designed with punishment or retribution in mind. Many times sisters enhanced children's spirituality or taught them important life lessons. One child caught throwing a candy wrapper to the ground learned to appreciate a clean environment after he was charged with picking up garbage around the schoolyard. Another was instructed that, for every bit of trash she picked up, a lost soul was released from purgatory.

Other times, children were encouraged to make amends in ways that allowed them to improve academically, perhaps even help lead them toward a life's calling. After writing more than her fair share of thousand-word essays beginning with "Why it's my responsibility to ____," one seventh grader grew up to become a writer.

Many nuns jumped on B. F. Skinner's bandwagon and introduced positive reinforcement into their discipline arsenal. Sisters embraced rewarding good behavior and delighted in handing out holy cards, rosary beads, and trinkets "blessed by Father."

They also figured out children lapped up attention lavished on them when assigned special jobs. Sisters saw no need to appoint line leaders or volunteers to run the attendance list to the office because students rarely got out of line or missed school. Nuns simply created new duties. For good behavior, students earned the privilege of taking out trash or straightening books in the library. For exceptional behavior, children were asked to clean the convent. Even though activities centered on manual labor, most children looked upon them as rewards because, as one man quipped, "It kept you out class and away from the nuns."

Much has been discussed in literature and in the movies about how strict nuns were, but their reasons for tough love are rarely addressed. Indeed, hindsight may produce shock and even criticism over their actions but in all fairness, nuns and their students lived by standards different than those in place today. Sisters taught during an era when "politically correct" meant knowing the proper way to address the president. A spare-the-rod-spoil-the-child approach to raising children prevailed full-force in both private and public schools.

Nuns didn't operate in a vacuum, either. Most pre-1970s parochial schoolchildren understood sisters had full support of parents. A Sister-picked-on-me whine more likely was greeted with a whack on the bottom from Dad than an offer to speed-dial the principal. Robert McQueen remembers his dad, who had great respect for the women who taught the eight McQueen children, often instructing the nuns: "If they get out of line, just hit them."

Why were sisters so exacting? A simple, "That's the way we were taught to teach," was how one nun justified herself. Right. Envision a classroom full of young novices hunched over their writing pads jotting notes describing which technique worked better for gaining children's attention: back-thumping or hair-pulling.

"We were instructed to teach that God is a fearful God, not a loving God as we know Him today," she explained. That tidbit, along with knowing a nun's most important teaching duty was to lead her children to heaven, gave new meaning to the expression "beat the hell out of you."

Regardless of how iron-fisted nuns seemed at the time, recollections today reflect genuine respect for them and often convey a sense of gratitude. Strict measures taught the children self-discipline, respect, and accountability, traits not often learned in many modern classrooms. Sisterly tough love is often remembered fondly and many times viewed as a Catholic badge of honor.

DISCIPLINE MEMORIES

Beyond Rulers: Weapons of Choice

Head Patrol

Sisters stood outside the church door checking to see that all the girls' heads were covered. Those attempting to sneak by found themselves yanked back by the strap on their uniform jumper or, worse yet, by their ponytails. By the seventh grade, most girls had learned to cut their hair or wear it up to avoid this hazard.

The Artful Dodge

Sister Mary Gregory liked to smack kids on their palms or calves with a long belt-like cloth strap that dangled from the waistband of her habit. It was handy; no need to search for a ruler or pointer.

Because I had been on the receiving end of Sister's swinging strap more than a couple of times, I had developed a keen sense of agility in attempts to avoid full-force swatting. During one particular lashing, Sr. Mary Gregory pulled the strap back, gearing up to strike a massive hit on my hand. I pulled my hand out of the strap's path, only to hear a pop followed by a loud groan. Sister hit herself! Doubled over in pain, she ordered me to bring my mother to her after school.

The next day, Sr. Mary Gregory called me to the front of the room.

"I owe you an apology," Sister said.

She owed me an apology?

"Your mother pointed out to me that since the strap was part of my habit, it was wrong of me to desecrate the holy cloth by striking you with it," Sister explained.

A ruler would have been okay?

Little Joe

"Little Joe," standing a mere four foot ten and presumably in her seventies, was a powerhouse beneath her flowing black Sisters of Charity habit. She handled us fifth graders in a straightforward, sometimes scary, manner. Stabbing us repeatedly in our chests with her bony index finger was one of her favorite attention-getting techniques.

No More Yardsticks
I attended Catholic grade school during the late forties and early fifties and was taught by the Sisters of Mercy. Most of these nuns maintained discipline using either a ruler or yardstick. Sometimes both. The implements seemed as much a part of their habits as were their black head-dresses.

The palms of my hands were nearly worn out from whacks by the time I reached seventh grade. I wasn't going to take it anymore.

Enough is enough, I thought as Sister approached me with her yardstick. I grabbed it out of her hand and cracked it in half over my knee. No more yardstick for me!

Sister didn't say anything; she only smiled. She never came after me with a yardstick or ruler again. The following year in eighth grade, no rulers or yardsticks were used.

Thank you, Sister. I guess there are no yardsticks in heaven, are there?

Attention Getter
Sister was a good teacher but her distinctive discipline measures worried us kids. One of her favorite methods for getting our attention was throwing the eraser or piece of chalk at a kid—and she never missed. Sister had an arm enviable by any major-league baseball team.

For those days when she needed to get the entire class's attention, she used her dime-store clicker. Funny how those contraptions had the strangest way of disappearing! Eventually, Sister tied the clicker to her habit, right alongside her rosary beads.

Horse Blinders
Some of the good nuns in the Italian Filippini order who taught us were deceptively young, not yet twenty years old but impossible to tell for certain under those formidable habits. Others were quite el-

derly. I will go to my death remembering my second-grade teacher, Sr. Mary Leo. She was one battle-axe of a nun! One day Sr. Mary Leo caught Gary Hendle cheating on a test. For his punishment, she created a set of cardboard horse blinders and forced him to wear them during exams. I can't even begin to imagine a teacher today trying to force a student to wear such a contraption.

Promotion

Sister Hubert was the Mother Superior of corporal punishment. Rumor had it she smashed one holy terror's head into the blackboard. Although that's never been proven, there *was a crack* in the board.

One morning, Sister Hubert asked us to take out our penmanship books. To my horror, I couldn't find mine. *Think, think, think,* my mind raced. Got it! I grabbed my book with Bible stories and pretended to read. Sister couldn't be angry with me for that, right? Wrong.

"Where's your penmanship book, sonny?" Sister said. Boys were always "sonny" and girls, "missy."

"Sister, I don't have it but...." She stopped me before I could get another word out. Sister grabbed my book and *attempted to smash it on my head.*

Fortunately, a quick left arm and a lucky block saved me. No advancement notice was ever as special as the one that read, "PROMOTED TO 4th GRADE."

Sign Her Up

Sister Margaret Richard should have tried out for the Pittsburgh Pirates. Her throwing arm was as strong and accurate as that of any professional baseball player. She hurled books, chalkboard erasers, whatever was nearby, to get students' attention or even to wake up those who took the chance to doze in class. Her aim came in handiest when squirting us with her always-loaded water pistol, sometimes shooting from across the room.

Beyond Rulers: Object Lessons

Making Faces

I always had trouble with nuns and they had trouble with me. As punishment for cutting up in class, I was required to kneel on the floor behind Sister as she sat at her desk in the front of the room. I faced my classmates but Sister had her back to me, an ideal situation for me to entertain the other kids and not get caught. I pulled my ears, stuck out my tongue, made faces, and did just about anything to cause the other kids to laugh. This infuriated Sister even further but what did she expect me to do when she placed me in front of the room? Pray?

Setting an Example

When I was in first grade, a misbehaving eighth-grade boy was remanded to our class because of his juvenile behavior. In the hopes of humiliating him, Sister made the boy suffer the indignity of squeezing into one of our tiny desks for the day. It worked. We couldn't stop staring and giggling.

Sister Bulldog

Schedules were mixed up my senior year. It turns out that thirty-five of us boys weren't assigned a required history class and all established classes were full. We were placed into a first-year teacher's open class period the last hour of the day.

Chaos ruled, until the day we waved the Good Humor truck over to the classroom window. Money flew out the window and ice creams flew in. Mother Superior stepped in to instill classroom order.

Mother, nicknamed "Bulldog" because of her uncanny resemblance to that canine breed, ordered us to stay after school. We placed our history books on top of our desks, then folded our hands and laid them on top of the books. We were to spend two hours sitting upright looking straight ahead while "Bulldog" strolled up and down the aisles brandishing her yardstick.

She alternated between lecturing us and cruising in silence. None of us spoke a word or turned our heads. Near the end of the two hours, tension was thick and nerves were frayed. Dick Golonka changed that.

As Mother passed Dick sitting in the front seat of the middle row, he lifted his history book high in the air for all behind him to see.

Schoolbooks in the 1960s were wrapped in shiny protective covers sold at the local pharmacy, usually showcasing a university's name on the front and its mascot on the back. Dick's history-book cover featured Yale University. Waved directly in front of us thirty-five tortured teenage boys was a drawing of that university's mascot—a snarling Bulldog, incisors hanging from its mouth, wearing a Yale beanie cap.

We erupted into laughter and Mother ran up and down the aisles whacking us with her yardstick. The more she smacked us the harder we laughed, further infuriating her.

We spent the next afternoon with her in that classroom, books and hands on top of our desks, sitting in silence. That time, we did it right.

Pockmarked Boy

Throwing an eraser at a nun was a major offense in 1941. The deed not only merited an exacting punishment, but an audience as well. For those of us chosen as spectators—unsuspecting first graders in our first week of school—the experience was akin to those of peasants herded into the town square for the public hanging of some poor wretch. I sat in quiet horror as two petite nuns dragged an older boy into our classroom. He must have been in eighth grade because he wore knickers while we younger boys still wore shorts. He towered over the nuns.

Each nun gripped one of his arms with one hand and clutched a ruler in her free hand. The boy twisted and thrashed, yet couldn't break free of their stronghold. They positioned him squarely in the front of the classroom, one on his right arm and the other on the left arm, creating a human cross.

"This is what can happen to you," the tinier Sister told us. I melted into my desk.

In unison, the women smacked the poor brute's exposed calves. He hopped as they whacked, jumping up and down in a Mexican hat dance. By the time the nuns finished with him his calves were marked with rectangle ruler imprints. We were duly impressed.

The following day a new boy entered our grade. We were all bug-eyed with wonderment as he stepped into our classroom. On our new classmate's face were two very large, red rectangle pockmarks, one on each cheek. Whatever did the young boy do to raise the nuns' ire in a manner that resulted in such a deformity, we wondered. We soon learned his facial malformation was the result of a bout with chicken pox and not nuns.

Thick As Thieves

Sister Michael inspired awe, fear, and admiration. The woman had the face of an angel that topped a six-and-a-half-foot frame. Her stature rivaled that of the largest linebackers Notre Dame had to offer. She was intelligent, articulate, and taught us both math and religion with a flaming passion. I believe she was a gentle soul but, because of her size, she served as the school's official disciplinarian.

By the time I was in the upper grades, I had been with the same group of boys since arriving at Holy Name in the second grade. We were as close to a band of brothers that you could find, sticking by each other through thick and thin. We played sports, served in the Boy Scouts, fought and befriended each other over and over again. Even after we parted ways to become archrivals attending different Catholic high schools, we remained close friends because of our years at Holy Name.

When we hit eighth grade, we knew the school bell system as well as we knew each other. Ten seconds before the recess bell rang, we counted down ten-nine-eight-seven. . . . We emptied the classroom, half of us running out the door and the other half jumping out of the first-floor windows. Every day, Sister shook her head and gave us a look but she really didn't mind our rambunctious maneuvers. The only time we didn't use the windows was at the end of the day when it was our job to lock them up for the night. Well, almost the only time. We left one unlocked on Fridays.

About five or six of us enjoyed sneaking back into the school Friday nights just to experience the thrill of being there without any teachers. We didn't steal or destroy anything, we just walked around the school as if we were James Bond spies knowing the nuns were right next door in the convent connected to the school.

Word of our Friday excursions leaked out and each week more and more of our classmates showed up at the school. As the crowds grew, things starting getting out of hand. The night of our final trip, there were twenty boys from the two eighth-grade classes and they wreaked havoc. Candy canes were ripped from the first-grade bulletin boards by some of the kids while others wrecked the school Christmas tree and broke ornaments. I'm not proud of that night and many of us tried to prevent the hooliganism but the trip had turned into a nightmare; it was only going to get worse.

It was a miracle the nuns didn't hear us and call the police. Sister Michael was astute, however. The following Monday, she called my buddy into the office and told him she knew he had been in the school. Who else was with him, she demanded. Feeling trapped, my buddy admitted there were a "few" others. Sister Michael told him to round up all the offenders and show up in her classroom at the end of the day. We all knew that meant suspension or even expulsion.

When Sister stepped into the classroom, all sixty boys in the eighth grade greeted her. Without being asked, every boy showed up, even the honor students and goodie-two-shoes. The boys all stood together, willing to accept our punishment.

Sister faced a quandary. She couldn't expel the entire class but we needed disciplining. Everyone would get a swatting, she decided.

Each of us was to receive three swats. Now, three swats doesn't sound like too much but the usual punishment for a serious offense was only one swat; on rare occasions two swats were meted out. Three swats amounted to a death sentence.

Sixty students were too many for Sister to tackle alone so she called in another teacher, a man we nicknamed Mr. Welt-dale because of the way he handled a solid hickory pointer. Mr. Welt-dale took half of the boys and left the other half to Sr. Michael and her "exterminator"—a five-foot paddle six inches wide with holes drilled into it. I was in Sister's group, which, considering her size, may not have been a lucky move for me.

We lined up at the "starting position," bent over and grabbed our ankles so that Mr. Welt-dale and Sister could take proper aim. It took longer for Sister to finish because each of us had to pick ourselves off the floor on the other side of the room and walk back to the starting position after each swat.

I realize this sounds like a brutal horror story, but Sister really saved our lives. She could have called the police and we would have been charged with trespassing and vandalism. Expulsion from school would have been the least of our worries. Instead, she taught me a lesson I still remember nearly forty years later. It was more effective than any jail sentence could have been. The incident was never mentioned again, not even to our parents. We were wrong, admitted it, were punished, and forgiven. The *Baltimore Catechism* never gave a better lesson than Sr. Michael.

Beyond Rulers: Fitting the Crime

This Is the Way We Iron Our Book
In the seventh grade I was taught religion by a nun built like a bulldog. We affectionately called her Sr. Bullface, behind her back, of course. Sister Bullface taught lessons in faith from that famed, universal text used by all Catholic-school students—the *Baltimore Catechism*. I hurriedly opened my copy one morning and accidentally wrinkled the first page of the book. It was a mess. Sister Bullface discovered the mess and barked at me to go home and fix it. How do you do that, I wondered?

Well, I did it the way my mother took out wrinkles in clothes—with an iron! I pulled out my mother's iron and ironing board and tried pressing out the page. As hard as I worked, some wrinkles never came out. I like to tease new acquaintances that due to my Catholic-school training I now work in a tailor shop and am head presser.

Spitting Boy
The fine art of spitting came so easily to Tony Petroli that he decided to share his talents with the rest of his schoolyard buddies one after-noon. That was not a good thing because Sr. Rosemary, our sixth-grade teacher, caught him in the act. For his punishment, Tony was forced to kneel in front of the classroom and spit continuously into the trash can until the dismissal bell rang. He wasn't allowed to drink any water; he just spat, spat, spat. I'm pretty sure he gave up the practice after that.

Spitball Jars
Billy loved shooting spitballs but was not very secretive when firing off the wet wads. Sister caught him one day and warned him, "If you spit one more spitball, you'll be made to fill an entire jar with them."

Naturally, Billy gave it another shot. And true to her word, Sister made Billy fill an entire jar with those disgusting gobs of gooey paper. The sight made a lasting impression on me.

Beyond Rulers: Mind Games

Spanking Machine
Sister Michael Francis, our principal at St. Jerome's grade school, was a large and imposing woman who wasn't shy about using fear to keep us little tykes in line. She claimed to have a spanking machine in her office and threatened to use it if we misbehaved.

One morning as I was walking past her office, I sneaked a quick peek inside. There, on a table, was an awful-looking contraption that surely must have been Sister's spanking machine! It had a metal base and a steel lever that I assumed was the spanking arm. The machine frightened me so badly that I never told anyone I had seen it. I went on to become a star pupil, even promising to become a nun one day.

Today I can laugh at myself because I realize the infamous spanking machine actually was a paper cutter. Years later I ran into Sr. Michael Francis, who had a good chuckle when I shared my memories with her.

Lie Detector

Our classrooms at St. Francis de Sales were not air-conditioned in the early '60s. Sr. Raymond turned on a huge fan and threw open all the windows, but still, some days there was nothing she could do to overcome our Louisiana heat and humidity. Those muggy, sticky ninety-degree temperatures usually drained the energy from most of us children but I think they drove one boy nearly crazy.

Larry was very active; today a doctor might label him hyperactive and prescribe him the drug Ritalin. In large doses. On particularly steamy days, Larry surprised and entertained the rest of us by jumping out of one of the windows and running around the schoolyard. Quick as a flash, though, Sr. Raymond darted out the doorway and ran after Larry, dragging him back into the room.

Chasing Larry in that heat surely must have been insufferable for Sr. Raymond as she was dressed head-to-toe in the traditional, itchy woolen habit of her order. Sister decided to put an end to his escapades.

"If you jump out the window again, I'll force you to undergo the lie-detector test."

What in the world was a "lie-detector test"? None of us knew. It must have been truly horrible. Sister spoke to us in hushed, ominous tones and her demeanor foreshadowed the severity of Larry's punishment if he hopped out the window again.

The threats effectively frightened Larry into remaining seated at his desk. He never jumped out of the window again. Air-conditioning eventually was installed at St. Francis de Sales, cooling both temperatures and temperaments.

Sincerely Yours

We were required to kneel in front of one old nun (geez, they all were old, it seemed) with our hands held together as if we were praying and say, "Please forgive me, Sister, for my rudeness." If she thought we were truly sorry, she patted us on the head and let us leave. If she doubted our sincerity she sent us to the office. The principal swung a mean paddle. We did our best to make our pleas sound genuine.

Playing with Teeth

The most impressive discipline tactic I have ever witnessed was one favored by Sister Isadore, my tenth-grade geometry teacher. She looked as if she spent most of her free time in a weight room and walked with a confident swagger that came from knowing none of us could outrun her.

Boys were required to wear dress shirts and ties to school. Sister would grab boys by their ties, yank them out of their seats, and pull their faces close to hers so she could whisper, "Ya wanna play with your teeth?"

Sister Isadore was a tough egg. No one ever got away with any nonsense in her class.

Disciplining Measures

The assistant principal at my high school had just finished disciplining me and I was walking back to class. I was disheartened and it must have showed on my face because one of the nuns stopped and asked me what was wrong. I told her how frustrated and angered I was over my punishment. Sister's words continue to ring out loud and clear thirty years later: "We discipline you so that you will learn self-discipline." Her comments didn't make a lot of sense to me then as a teenager, but as I grew so did the value of her statement.

Brotherly Love

My father, whose sister has been a nun since 1939, had great respect for the sisters at St. Phillip's teaching his eight children. He told them to smack us if we got out of line. And they did. All of us boys in my family received our share of those hard knocks. A few times, though, one of us would finagle a reprieve without Sister's knowledge.

When I was in the third grade, my brother Max was in the fourth grade and constantly in hot water. His teacher, Sr. Mary Edward, told him to bring his brother to her so that she could send a message home to our father. Max retrieved Steve, our brother in fifth grade.

Sister outlined all of Max's behavioral problems to Steve, who, being the oldest of our brood, thought it his responsibility to report the behavior problems to Dad. Max was soundly punished.

Since I was the third child and didn't share the same level of responsibility as Steve, Max fetched me the next time he got in trouble with Sr. Mary Edward. I couldn't bring myself to squeal on Max so I never told my father.

The next day at school, Sr. Mary Edward asked me if I told my father about Max's behavior. I told her that I did.

"What did he do?" she asked.

"He beat him."

"Good," Sister said as she sent me back to class, confident that my father indeed had dished out the correct measure of punishment.

From that day on, Max always came to me when he was in trouble with the sisters.

Finger Wagging

Sister Ignatius was in her eighties by the time she taught me. She was renowned for her finger wagging—pointing and shaking her index finger at us for the least bit of infractions of the rules. Sister could barely talk without shaking her finger.

Apparently, finger wagging must have been a lifelong habit for Sr. Ignatius, because the index finger on her right hand was notably longer than the rest of her fingers. Decades of wagging had loosened the joint and elongated her finger.

Sister-to-Be

Sister Loretta was my teacher for two years in a row and we locked horns many times. I think I was just about as stubborn as she. One day I provoked her. She ordered me on my knees and to pray I would become a nun. All I could think of at the time was "misery loves company."

Ruler Fee

Our eighth-grade teacher would strike our hands with a plastic ruler. Our hands reached outward, palm up or down depending on Sister's mood. Many times the ruler would break and we were forced to purchase Sister a new one—with our own money!

Beyond Rulers: Brute Force

Is it Sr. Jeckyll or Sr. Hyde?

Our morning routine was well underway. Sister Frances was berating us, tugging our ears, and pinching our necks when we heard a loud rap on the door.

"Gooood Mooorning, Faaather Schotts," we said, standing to welcome Father into our classroom.

"Sister, can you spare four altar boys to serve at a funeral with me?" he asked. Sister Frances pulled a Jeckyll and Hyde act. A smiling Sister Jeckyll selected me and three others to serve, kindly telling Father how we were "such nice young men."

We were happy for the few hours' respite but upon our return we were greeted by the loathsome Sr. Hyde who was busy scolding, tugging, and pinching. The power of a priest!

Faster Than a Whacking Ruler

Mother Superior caught my brother doing what he always was doing—the wrong thing! She told him to hold out his hands. He did. She brought the ruler down and, *whoosh*, he moved his hands. He laughed. She didn't.

She told him again to hold out his hands. He did and, *whoosh*, he moved them out of the way again. Again, he laughed. Infuriated, Mother Superior popped him on the head with the ruler. My brother, caught off guard, hollered and put his hands up to his head to rub the pain.

When his hands flew up to his head, Mother Superior brought the ruler down *whack, whack, whack,* turning his knuckles crimson red.

Hair-Raising, Desk-Raising Episode

Taking in the air around Sr. Alice was a lot like breathing in a linen closet. The closer she got to me, the more she reminded me of stored sheets. Sister was tall and stocky, too. As a first grader, I found her presence foreboding. And that was before I faced her rage during the "desk-raising" encounter.

Sister told us to take our readers out from the small cubbies under our desks. Allen, the boy in the desk next to mine, knelt in the aisle as he rummaged through his desk looking for his book. Sister Alice thundered to him to immediately find his book. A few seconds later she was at his side, and in an imitation of Frankenstein's monster hurling dogs and children, Sister picked up his desk, held it over her head, and shook the hell out of it. Out fell candy wrappers, gum, wadded-up papers, pencils, crayons, and even a collection of Matchbox cars. You name it and it fell out of that desk.

Heaving with rage, Sister's face turned beet red and she broke out in a sweat. After settling down for a moment, Sister Alice wiped her brow, revealing a permanent crease on her forehead formed by her habit. She walked away from Allen, rosary beads clicking and clacking at her side, and said nothing more than for him to pick up the mess.

My first experience with a nun's rage was very frightening. In fact, it remains a scary memory today, many years later.

Rewarding Birds

I was not a nice kid. Detentions and punishments were a way of life for me at Holy Name. I deserved most of what I got.

Once in the sixth or seventh grade, a sister whose name I have apparently blocked from my memory forced me to place my hands palms-down on my desk. She then whacked them with a long, rubber-tipped pointer.

As she turned and walked to her desk, I held back the pain, and in sheer adolescent bravado, "flipped her a bird" so that all in the class could see. When Sister reached her desk, she turned to the class and said, "Michael took his punishment well. He deserves candy."

Nap-Time Easter Eggs

Each afternoon, we first graders were required to rest by placing our heads on our desks and keeping our eyes closed. Sister Gertrude strolled up and down the aisles making sure we kept our heads down. That was a tough job for a few of us. One spring afternoon, Sister offered us candy Easter eggs as an incentive to keep our heads down. As she walked by each of us, she set an egg on our desk. We still were required to keep our heads down, though.

When a scented blend of sugary chocolate and sterile soap wafted up to my nose, I knew that Sister stood in front of my desk. I squirmed a bit but kept my head down. I was dying to see what color egg I had. I lifted my head and opened my eyes.

And there she was! Sister hadn't moved away from my desk. In a flash, she kicked my chair out from under me and there I lay on the floor just staring up at her. She took away my Easter-egg candy and kept me out of recess for two days. Talk about positive reinforcement!

At least I was more honest than the other kids. Most of them peeked, too. They just waited until Sister walked past them.

Priceless Pugilist

Sister Martin John had a very humane "two-warnings" approach to discipline with unspecified but implicitly dangerous consequences for three-peaters. One morning, Louis "call me Louie" Galdoni was irrepressible in a typically Brooklyn way—meaning loud. Louie sat in the desk behind me, one row over. Sister gave Louie his two warnings, usually enough to shut up anyone but for some reason, he continued yakking.

Sister Martin executed a flanking maneuver around the far wall of the classroom and stealthily approached him from behind. I saw her coming but my fear-widened eyes failed to warn him. Like the proverbial bolt from out of the blue, Sister smacked Louie upside the head with a right roundhouse. He let out a guttural noise of surprise and threw his arms up to protect his head just in time to catch her left roundhouse.

The beating continued, right, left, right, until Louie slumped forward and gave up. At that point, Sr. Martin ceased fire. She drew herself up to her full height, which couldn't be more than five foot two, and stalked wordlessly to the front of the room, now deathly quiet.

Total attack time: perhaps fifteen seconds. Impact on this witness: a lifetime. Lesson learned: don't irritate small women.

Chalkboard Duty
Sister Leo earned a reputation for being tough. One of my classmates, Sam, was writing a lesson on the chalkboard and apparently he wasn't performing quite up to Sister's standards. Sister Leo grabbed his neck, lifted him off the ground, and erased the board with him.

My mom always joked the sisters had eyes in the back of their habits because they seemed to catch wind of mischief while it was still in the making. My nuns may have had eyes in the back of their habits but they must have closed them when it came to me. I started out quiet and obedient, followed all the rules, and politely answered "yes, Sister." I blame it on hormones going berserk, but around the time I hit puberty I turned into Peter Finch acting out my own version of "I'm mad as hell and I'm not going to take it anymore."

I didn't do anything drastic like writing "drop dead, Sister" on the chalkboard the way Mary Ellen did. Even though I detested Sister's music class, I didn't go on a wilding and smash her guitar or rip out the keys in her piano the way Mark did. I certainly didn't bombard Sister with water balloons the last day of school the way the Martin sisters did. I just turned into a mouthy teenager. Or cheeky, as the nuns called me.

When given the task to present a report about the person we most admired, I said Sister gave us the assignment hoping we'd discuss her. Not willing to get sucked into that, I bypassed her as my choice, along with Pope Paul VI, my parents, and even the blessed Mother. Instead, I heaped praises on Alfred E. Neuman, the cartoon character gracing *MAD* magazine covers. This earned me the label "cheeky *and* impertinent."

Eventually, I gave up tormenting the nuns. But not before I learned a lot of different ways to call someone a smartass.

D. S.

I didn't participate in any of the hard-core pranks, knowing full well what would happen at home if I were caught. Instead, I chose the passive-aggressive/class-clown route. One sister, who apparently had just completed Psychology 101 at the junior college, informed me that I was retarded after one of my jokes backfired. This didn't bother me. First, I reasoned that if Sister didn't mean what she said, this was psychological warfare on both sides. Touché, Sister. If Sister was serious, I figured her slam didn't say too much for the school. By the time Sister made her arm-chair diagnosis I had made it through almost eight years.

M. P.

Chapter Seven

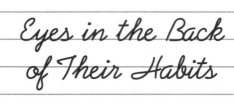

Eyes in the Back of Their Habits

CHUCKIE CARLSON TORE OFF A piece of notebook paper, wadded it up to the size of a pea, and stuck it in his mouth. Glancing over his shoulder to check on Sr. Gertrude's whereabouts and finding her two rows over, Chuckie pulled a small cylinder out of his shirt pocket.

"Holy Mary, pray for us. Mother of God, pray for us. Angels of God, pray for us," Sr. Gertrude intoned, strolling up and down the rows of students while leading them in petitions to the saints.

Just after Sister passed his desk, Chuckie drew the hollow tube to his mouth, took aim, and fired. Bull's-eye! He plastered a goopy spitball square on the back of Sr. Gertrude's veil. The white glob clung to the black fabric and hung there the entire morning. He thrilled his classmates, their whispered "attaboys" and admiring glances flowing in Chuckie's direction. The boy puffed up like a native felling an unsuspecting Johnny Weissmuller with a poison blow dart in an old Tarzan flick.

Recess bell rang and as Chuckie started to leave the room, Sister pulled him aside. She shoved a wastepaper basket in his hands. Sister Tarzan had feigned unconsciousness after Chuckie's attack, only to pounce on the native hero just as he was about to dance in jubilation with fellow tribesmen.

"Since small bits of paper intrigue you, help yourself to a whole school's worth," she said, holy smugness spreading across her face. Chuckie spent the afternoon picking up trash in the schoolyard.

As in Chuckie's case, there came a time in most Catholic school-children's lives when a burning desire to break away from nuns' authority overtook them. It dawned unexpectedly, an unseen bully standing behind them slowly pulling up the slack of their scapulars, until there was no slack left. Tossing halos to the wind, young angels-in-the-making fought the chokehold with an uprising. Many youths came to believe they *actually could* pull a fast one on the sisters. Holy card-toting Sodality of Mary girls and bell-ringing altar boys cratered, joining the ranks of hard-core troublemakers.

Formerly obedient, rule-abiding students crossed over to the dark side. After years of following unrelenting orders governing their every action, and enduring rigid discipline measures when they didn't, adolescents snapped. Even brown-nosing goody-two-shoes defected to an enemy camp, a place where kids actually had a good time. These young rebels gave in to their causes—humiliating, embarrassing, or teasing a sister—just because they could. Catholic-school James Deans emerged, reveling in their newly acquired thrill-seeker status.

To this day, Eddie Zukowski thinks about his former classmate Peter's deception and shakes his head in bewilderment. Zukowski recalled the day Peter gained access to the school's intercom system so that he could announce the whereabouts of Sr. Joseph, their teacher who was away for the day.

"Excuse me, I have sad news to report," Peter broadcast. "Sister Joseph has passed away."

Continuing uninterrupted, probably because students and staff alike were shell-shocked, Peter explained Sister's demise.

"It seems Sister wore her eighteen-hour girdle for nineteen hours."

Zukowski and his former classmates are still marveling at why Peter pulled his stunt, which led to his immediate expulsion. Most tricksters claim that boredom and not rebellion drove them to some of the best monkeyshines—and without their having to suffer severe repercussions.

Sister Adrian was a tad off-balanced, or so she seemed to Cory (McCallister) Barlow and her classmates at St. Sylvester's in Brooklyn. "We entertained ourselves at Sister's expense as often as we could," Barlow admitted. One trick employed was convincing Sister she was teaching a class of deaf-mutes.

"When Sister asked us a question, we mouthed the answer. Sister assumed because she couldn't hear us we couldn't hear her. The more we mouthed our answers, the louder she asked the questions."

"Sister Adrian crescendoed to a scream and we still didn't relent. She stormed out of the classroom in frustration, leaving us in a giggle fit," Barlow said.

Some students saw their uprisings as retaliation for the way a nun treated or spoke to them. Miffed by the nuns at her school, Mary Lou (Wilson) Habel organized a work strike. Wilson had just transferred to St. Cecelia's from a public school and was adjusting to the changes pretty well. Or so she thought, until the end of the week.

"Sister Agnes Mary told all of the girls to put on their aprons, which confused me. What aprons, I wondered. Sister handed me one, explaining that each Friday the eighth-grade girls scrubbed and waxed school floors."

The rest of the girls retrieved aprons from the cloakroom while the boys skipped outside to play baseball. Habel's astonishment quickly turned to anger—and action. She staged a walkout.

"Girls, this is *not* right. We're in here scrubbing while the boys play," Habel said, stoking fiery emotions with the finesse of a local teamsters rep. "Let's march over to Foxwood Pharmacy for an ice cream in protest."

To Habel's amazement, the other girls tossed their aprons aside and trekked to the pharmacy with her.

"I was a Gloria Steinem before there even was a Gloria Steinem," she chuckled. Of course, she and the girls had to answer to Sr. Agnes as well as to seven other nuns and the pastor when they returned.

Most high jinks were good-natured and harmless, like tormenting classmates with fake rubber vomit. However, tossing the toy onto a pew during the middle of Mass could be treacherous, especially when it distracted the priest. A young boy hid phony spew until it was time to kneel. As he slipped to his knees, he placed the bogus hurl on the seat behind him. Father had barely finished praying *sanctus, sanctus, sanctus* when a primal scream erupted from a row of girls spotting the pile of vomit.

Causing Father to get off track during the sacred ritual was enough to send nuns into orbit, which moved an innocent prank into the category of sin. How long and hard Father glared at Sister determined whether the sin was venial or mortal. The worst part to Sister was the child wasting his money on the toy when he could have sent it the missions.

Shenanigans often were conceived and plotted with the cunning of a military commander preparing to dispatch midnight sorties. One of the more devious tactics hatched by a class of teenage girls probably had one nun convinced she was losing her marbles. In a way she was but didn't know it.

Several girls tucked dozens of dime-sized glass beads into their pockets before entering the classroom. Once Sister began teaching, all the girls pulled out handfuls of beads and dropped them to the floor. With each bounce, *plink-plink-plink* resonated throughout the room. The clear balls melted into the mottled floor and rolled off into oblivion. Sister peered over glasses perched on the edge of her nose but couldn't find anything amiss. After a few more toss-downs, Sister's frenzy could have landed her the role as Ingrid Bergman's understudy in *Gaslight*.

Adolescent bombast earned one practical jokester a spot in the nun-anguish hall of fame. Accounts of his feat circulated faster than an Internet urban legend. Paul Deren remembers the day he and fellow eighth graders at St. James had front-row seats to a rare musical performance.

"Sister Raymond faced our class with her back to the door where we saw Timmy McAfee standing with a trumpet in his hand. He crept into the room until he was standing behind Sister," Deren said. "Timmy put that trumpet to his lips and blew a blast inches from her ear!"

Sister jumped ten feet in the air, according to Deren. Timmy bolted out of the room, down the hall, outside the building, and across the parking lot—with a seventy-year-old nun in pursuit.

"We cheered him on as we watched through the windows. Sister didn't catch him," Deren said. "At least not then."

For every piece of tomfoolery children attempted, quick-witted sisters crushed dozens more. Forget about fathers; sisters knew best. Or at least, they knew everything their students were up to, sometimes, it seemed, even before the kids did.

Sisters were known for gliding up and down rows of desks with their hands clasped in front of them and heads facing forward, never veering left or right. They floated by in a meditative trance while students busied themselves with coursework. Yet, let one student try passing a note behind sister's back—he earned himself a ticket on the back-thumping express the next time the nun cruised down his row.

Reports like these confirm decades-old suspicions: nuns had eyes in the back of their habits. Or at least spy gear. Under her habit's bib, Sister might have hidden a miniature spy monocular that she could slip into her palm when pulling out a hankie. Most kids thought Sister's piety drove her to bow her head and bring her clasped hands to her face in prayer but she was probably scanning the playground with the latest surveillance technology.

Maybe it wasn't spy gear but psychic consulting that gave nuns their edge. Every morning just before entering the classroom, sisters might have tapped into a student spy ring to get the scoop. Rumors spread that some children might actually have been psychic tattle-tales.

"Oooh, I see big cloud of trouble headed your way, Sister, and it's gonna dump a rain shower on you if you're not careful," little Cleo, a foreign-exchange student from Jamaica, might have whispered.

"Hmm, must be the Fratella boy. He seemed a bit too eager yesterday when I told him to water the church garden. I better check where he placed the hose. Knowing him, it's hung over the entranceway. Thanks, Miss Cleo."

"Oh, no problem. Talk to you tomorrow."

Sisters uncovered many capers because they were shrewd and, frankly, unorthodox. They exacted their own brand of wisdom, taking measures that would have left King Solomon scratching his head. These women were astute, too, understanding how to cool tempers and defuse explosive situations before they turned harmful.

When two young boys started a schoolyard brawl after a year of hostility mounting between them, Sr. Lucretia allowed them to duke it out instead of reporting the boys to the principal. The fisticuffs released tension and allowed them to get along with each other for the rest of the year.

Sometimes a nun's foresight might not have been appreciated for years to come, like the time a young boy was caught trading baseball cards in church during the '50s. The boy and his buddies figured out that by trimming the cards just so, they could slip them under a holy card. The boys passed the cards up and down the row, trading a St. Jude for a St. Anthony and a Sacred Heart of Jesus card for the both of them. They were convinced Sister was none the wiser. That was, until Sister whispered in the boy's ear, "You really shouldn't trim those cards. They may be valuable one day."

Truer words were never spoken. Among the boy's stash lay a Mickey Mantle rookie card worth nothing more than interest in 1952. Fifty years later, the card would have fetched as much as $50,000—had it been untrimmed.

It's hard to believe, but a few kids *did* get away with outrageous stunts, sometimes with a little help from the Church itself. Lou, Holy Redeemer's rogue-in-residence, wouldn't let the solemnity of a funeral keep him from raising a little hell. As an altar boy, he routinely served at funeral masses where he often pretended to cry. Actually, he sobbed loudly, heaved his shoulders, and occasionally wailed. A buzz spread throughout the congregation:

"Look at that little boy, he's so upset."

"He must have known him well."

"That poor child."

Lou usually didn't know the deceased.

As much as they wanted to hurdle the pew and yank Lou off the altar, nuns couldn't get within twenty feet of him. Before Vatican II reforms, women weren't allowed to stand on the church's altar. Contrary to schoolyard musings, nuns are women and even they, among the most loyal and holy in God's army, were unable to foil all altar-boy mischief.

Often a master prankster herself, a nun's own ability to pull a gag kept her a step or two ahead of students. In one all-girl Catholic orphanage, Sr. Grace was charged with waking up an older student, who in turn woke up the younger girls. The older student was a deep sleeper and Sister couldn't rouse her—until she squirted Sleeping Beauty with a water gun.

With eyes twinkling, sisters often carried out stunts with the help of carefully chosen students who usually were the most wearisome rabble-rousers in their classes. Through her collaborative trickery, Sr. Angela maintained class order and kept a troubled youngster in tow.

Sister Angela had a difficult time playing Sr. Tough Cookie but gave it her best shot with Andrew. Almost daily, Sister clutched a towering pointer in one hand, the scruff of Andrew's neck in the other, and dragged him off to the cloakroom, recalled Bonnie O'Malley. Once in the closet, Andrew screamed for mercy with each thwack reverberating from the room. After a few minutes, he emerged tear-stained and remorseful.

"Horror-struck, the rest of us watched in disbelief as our beloved Sr. Angela cast aside her normal calm and tenderness to turn into a cruel fiend. At least, that's what we thought," O'Malley said.

The good sister couldn't bring herself to strike the boy. Instead, she cut a deal with him.

"Every time I whack these coats, you yell loud and long," she told him inside the room. Soon, Andrew learned the routine and he and Sr. Angela had a laugh at the expense of the other kids. It was their special secret. Eventually, Andrew, like a cornered monkey in a zoo, jabbered away to the other kids. Afterward, each day someone begged to be disciplined by sister in her magical cloakroom.

Too often, nuns are thought to have been mean, overbearing, and humorless. Their classes were boring and earmarked by drudgery with students and sisters alike toiling a daily grind. Nothing could be further from the truth. Catholic students, like any other kids, delighted in a good time. Nuns enjoyed having fun, too. Whether due to rebellious natures, raging hormones, or a simple desire to skip class work, kids (and nuns, too) never shied away from having a few laughs with each other.

HAVING-FUN-WITH-A-NUN MEMORIES

Sisters and Shenanigans: Making Mischief

Changing Times
I was among one of the first "younger" altar boys to serve Mass, assisting Father every morning by the time I was a fifth grader. Paul and I were best buddies, hanging around and usually serving Mass together.

Paul nagged me to let him ring the bells, complaining that I always grabbed them. I said, "Okay, go ahead," and let him ring his heart out. After tinkling the bells, he left them on the steps near the altar. When Mass ended and everyone was clearing out of church, Paul went back to the altar to retrieve the priest's prayer book. Instead of going around the railing in front of the altar, Paul climbed over it and knocked over the bells with a resounding clang.

Seated in the front row praying after-Mass meditations and witnessing Paul's gymnastics were four very shocked nuns. As much as the sisters might have wanted to ring Paul's bell, they couldn't do a thing. Back then, women weren't allowed to step on the altar.

Holiday Wrapping
The old saying "kids will be kids" was especially true when pulling a stunt on a nun. My elderly sixth-grade nun frequently asked students to brush off the back of her veil and habit after she had leaned against the blackboard while teaching. During the Christmas season one year,

some of us thought it would be a nice touch if we added bows to her habit while flicking off the chalk. We brushed with one hand and stuck bows on the back of her head with the other. Sister couldn't understand why we giggled like a bunch of amused monkeys every time she turned her back to the class. After returning to the classroom from lunch in the convent, Sister still had the bows stuck to her headgear. Apparently the other nuns enjoyed the prank as much as we did.

Cup Runneth Over

Because we had good grades and could afford to miss a class, my best friend and I were sometimes asked to go to the convent and hang out the freshly laundered clothes on the line. One day, we had a load of underwear in the laundry basket. Nuns' underwear!

First we giggled but then we laughed when we pulled a bra out of the basket that surely must have belonged to Mother Superior. I had never seen a bra that large in my life. It hung from the clothesline and touched the ground. The cups looked large enough to put on my head—so I did!

Forevermore, we lovingly referred to Mother Superior as Mother Milk Duds.

Mystery Clicker

We had the utmost respect for sisters in their dark, flowing habits but one nun drove us nuts with a strange clicking sound floating from her habit. We always heard the *click, click, click* during recess. That was our signal to line up and walk like little robots into the classroom, where we remained until dismissal. A boy in our class must have seen Sister secretly slip the magical noisemaker into her desk because the moment she told us to make the sign of the cross on our lips—her unspoken sign she would be leaving the room and for us to remain silent—he hopped out of his seat and headed straight for her desk drawer.

Lo and behold, he discovered a tiny metal clicker shaped like a frog. The noise came from a toy, not Sister's magic. But the spell was broken. Sister was human. We were proud of our brave young companion to risk getting caught, which would have meant suffering Sister's wrath. We urged him to go to confession, though.

Loose Chicks

Because Sister Devota was sweet-natured, and sometimes forgetful, she found herself at the mercy of class pranksters. Once a group of boys put a dozen chicks—baby chickens—in Sister's top desk drawer. Where they got them, the rest of us never knew.

Sister opened the drawer and the chicks jumped out, peeping as they scattered about the room. Poor Sr. Devota scurried after the chicks but the tiny creatures eluded capture. The students burst out in delirious laughter! The boys finally came forward to help her catch the chicks and to our amazement, no one was punished.

Knockout

Sister Frances was impressive. Tall and intimidating, Sister routinely disciplined us eighth graders by pulling our ears, squeezing our necks, and slapping our knuckles with her ruler. One day, Sr. Frances pulled Johnny Latanzi's ear and he suddenly stood up. With a clenched fist, he drew back, yelled, "I've had enough of your shit," and sucker-punched her in the gut. Johnny jumped out of the classroom window and landed on the bushes. Then off he ran. The rest of us wanted to laugh because we thought she deserved it. But we didn't. I guess we felt sorry for her because she really had the wind knocked out of her. She was actually rolling around on the floor!

A Sweet Treasure Hunt

As a student in a Catholic boarding school in the 1940s, I had more experiences with nuns outside of a classroom than I would have had if I had attended a day school. Among those were my nightly excursions exploring the sisters' living quarters.

In the middle of the night, a group of three or four of us girls would awaken and sneak through a tunnel that led to the convent. We'd find our way to the kitchen pantry where we discovered a horde of cakes, pies, cookies, and other desserts. The only desserts served to us students were apples and oranges, never anything as delectable as the hidden treasure in the nuns' pantry.

The desserts were stale, but we didn't care. We carted our bounty back to the dormitory, where we stuffed ourselves silly. After months of nightly plundering, we were caught by Sr. Thomas who was up late working on the school yearbook. She reported us to the Headmistress, who called us thieves because we stole their treats. We spent the next two weeks at evening Angelus, kneeling upright in the middle of the church on hard marble floors for one hour each night.

Since we were thieves, we were expected to confess our sin to Fr. Parker. He heard my confession and asked if I took the food because I was hungry. I answered yes. He explained that since I was hungry, I hadn't really sinned. Hurrah! I wasn't going to hell for my pilfering! However, I did stop the secret trips to the pantry.

Sisters and Shenanigans: Pulling Wool Over Their Eyes

Good Girls Read Bibles

The nuns were so pleased with us girls at religious retreats. We thrilled them by devotedly reading our Bibles for hours on end. Thank goodness they didn't actually look inside the books to see what we were reading. Instead of seeing chapters and verses, they would have found *Seventeen* and *Tiger Beat* magazines.

Bless Those Poor Souls

Sister Dymphna was very old. Of course, I was a teenager and everyone looked old to me. Sister had such a kind heart but we naughty girls exploited that every chance we could.

Each time Sister heard a fire engine or police siren wail, she glanced toward the window and muttered, "Bless those poor souls." Trying to rid ourselves of boredom one slow morning, a few of us in the back let out a distant-sounding *Whooo, Whooo, Whooo.*

Sure enough, Sr. Dymphna turned around and intoned, "Bless those poor souls." We wailed again. She halted her lesson in full-sentence and prayed again. We wailed one more time and Sister uttered the blessing one more time. We kept the teasing up for nearly an hour. Tormenting Sr. Dymphna was a sure-fire way to beat boredom.

Rubber-Band Girl

I sat in the front row quietly reading my assignment along with my classmates. I passed the time fiddling with a rubber band, stretching it back and forth. It suddenly sprang from my hand and hit Sister Mary Evelyn squarely on the chest!

She didn't say a word. In fact, because of all the layers in her habit, she never felt the impact. The most humorous part was seeing the looks of amazement on my classmates' faces. In their eyes, my feat was sure to go down in St. Peter's history. I had shot a nun with a rubber band and got away with it!

Ring Those Bells

Recognizing us as the thug-types we were, Sister Hildegard ordered my buddies and me to sit in the front row so she could keep an eye on us. One of her favorite techniques for maintaining control was ringing a bell.

One particularly slow morning, Sister turned her back to us to write on the chalkboard. As soon as her back was turned, I grabbed the bell off her desk and unclasped the dinger. In a flash, I put it back on the desk and my buddies started shuffling their feet, trying to draw her attention to the rising commotion.

Sister Hildegard turned, picked up the bell, and shook it. Nothing happened. She shook it harder. Still nothing, so she put it back on her desk. Sister turned her back to us and we swiped the bell again, this time re-attaching the dinger. We then created a ruckus so she would turn around and grab the bell. She picked up the bell and shook it, and it rang loud and clear. Sister Hildegard hesitated, as if recalling that only moments before her bell hadn't worked.

Sister set the bell down and returned to the chalkboard. Once again, I grabbed the bell and removed the dinger while my buddies made noise. True to form, Sister turned around again, picked up the bell, and shook it. When it didn't ring, she just stared at it. We kept it up the entire class period. Sister Hildegard never figured it out.

Fireworks

We nicknamed one of our nuns "Scooter" because instead of walking she scooted down the hallways. Scooter had to be in her eighties and she wore eyeglasses with thick lenses.

One day, my last-period science teacher asked if any of us wanted a little fun after school. We agreed and then spent the rest of class making several homemade "snaps," those fireworks that let out a loud pop but no fire when tossed around at July Fourth celebrations.

Before the bell rang, we placed the snaps in the corridor outside our room and waited for the hallways to fill with students. We were excited to see reactions when the pops exploded.

The fireworks were in place, we had five minutes to go before dismissal, and along came Scooter. She was headed in our direction, bending over and picking up trash without stopping. She was headed toward our pops! Our teacher ran out in front of her, broom in hand, and swept the pops into a dustpan. We were lucky none exploded. So was Scooter.

Alarming Nuns

Our librarian, a nun we called "Sr. Broom Hilda," insisted on silence. To us little kids, she struck us as a crabby old lady. My buddy and I decided to liven things up. We collected four Baby Ben alarm clocks and synchronized them to go off at two-minute intervals. My friend and I hid them among the books in different corners of the library and then we headed off to our next class.

Five minutes later, the first of the four alarms went off. So did Sister! Two minutes later the second bell rang. In less than ten minutes, Sister went ballistic, scrambling around the library trying to find the ringing bells, according to kids still in the library. Although we never told anyone else about our escapade, we heard the accolades school-mates bestowed on the unknown tricksters. Rumor had it the entire student body wanted to present an award to the person/s who pulled off the stunt. Since that happened in 1978, I think it might be safe to come forward and accept the award now.

Spring Forward

Our elderly nun's classroom lights could be dimmed and the windows were covered by sun-blocking drapes. While Sister was out of the room, two of us pulled down the shades and another turned down the lights. We then set her classroom clock forward two hours. Sister glanced at the clock when she entered the room and, startled by the time, told us to leave.

"Oh my, students, your parents will be worried sick about you! Run, run, go home. Class dismissed."

We were slapped with a week's detention.

I Can't Hear You!

An elderly nun who taught high school was nearly deaf, and gullible, too. For fun, we often removed the clacker from the bell that rested on her desk. Sister picked up the bell and shook it hard, ringing it so we would pay attention. She didn't hear anything but all of us sat up-right and looked straight ahead—as if we had heard the ringing.

Other times, Sister would call on one of us to answer a question. The student mouthed an answer. "You children need to learn to speak up," Sister said each time we pretended to speak.

Hurdling Nun

My high school and St. Augustine were archrivals. We took every chance we could to get St. Augustine students into trouble. We learned that if anyone pulled the fire alarm there, the nuns slapped the entire student body with detention. During lunchtime one day, my buddies and I cruised over to our nemesis with the intention of sneaking in and pulling the fire alarm.

My job was to get into the school, pull the alarm, and take off running to our getaway car. Getting in was pretty easy. I crept along the walls until I found an alarm. Crouching, I reached my hand upward and just as I touched the lever, I looked over my shoulder to see if all was clear. It wasn't. Standing down the hall about twenty feet was a nun, hands on her hips, watching me. Uh-oh. Do I pull it or do I run out of there? I figured since I was already there, what the heck. I pulled and the siren wailed.

I bolted down the hallway with the nun following in hot pursuit. I dashed through the student parking lot and ran through the adjacent field. Sister was still chasing me, full speed. I ran harder and approached a fence about three feet high. Without slowing, I jumped, easily clearing the fence. I slowed to a trot, thinking I had outdistanced Sister who was running in her long dress and veil.

Turning back for one last look, I saw Sister hiking up her dress and charging toward me. Despite the full habit and headdress, Sister cleared the fence in full-hurdle formation. I took off running and jumped into the car. She never reached me but she did get close enough to record the license plate.

The Lineman

Sister Paul was in the middle of conducting our annual Christmas program, directing children onstage in the church while the rest of us waited our turn in the social hall, located directly behind the sacristy. Her shows were marathon productions, keeping kids and parents hostage for hours. This year's production didn't look any shorter.

I was in the eighth grade and our class was scheduled last, which meant hours spent sitting and waiting. Boredom settled in and a few of the guys went snooping. They discovered a box in the back alley filled with custodial supplies including several rolls of aluminum tape. Jackie grabbed one, unraveled it a bit and threw it in the air. The silvery tape glistened as it sailed under the lamppost. Cool, he and the others thought, so they unraveled more and kept tossing them into light's rays.

Snap. One of the rolls hit the power line, letting off a sparkling burst of electricity.

Double cool! Jackie and two of the boys threw more, this time *aiming* for the wires. Occasionally, they hit the line and sparks lit up the alley. Suddenly, two rolls hit a wire at the same time. *Kaboom, crackle, pop, pop, pop* filled the air and a fireworks display illuminated the night sky. Then nothing. The social hall, church, school, and all the houses for as far as we could see were blanketed by darkness. Within minutes, the sirens of fire trucks and emergency vehicles broke the back-alley quiet. Terrified, the boys slipped back into the hall.

It turns out Jackie and his buddies took out a transformer, leaving the church and the surrounding community without electricity for several hours. Sister had no recourse but to cancel the remaining performances. Parents, weary from the program already, believed the darkness was brought on by a divine act.

No one ever discovered how the lights went out and, upon reaching adulthood, Jackie went to work with the local light company, where he remains twenty-five years later.

Sisters and Shenanigans: Can't Fool Sister

Car or Nun Trouble?

My best buddy and three of his friends skipped Latin class. The boys strolled into school later in the day and told Sister Edwina that on the way to school their car broke down because of a flat tire. She looked at each boy and said, with a little hesitance, "Okay," and then apologized to them for what would come next.

Sister sent each of the now-nervous boys to a corner desk and told them to pull out a sheet of paper and write the answers to these questions: Which tire went flat? Where were you? Who jacked up the car? Where did you wash your hands?

The boys looked around the room to each other and knew they were busted. My buddy said it was the last time he ever told a lie.

Smoking Girls

As a student of Catholic schools for twelve years, I learned ignoring rules often resulted in a run-in with some real tough cookies dressed in black habits. That didn't stop me from pushing the limits, however.

At St. Maria Goretti High School, we weren't allowed to leave school grounds during the day. One afternoon my friend Kris and I sneaked out for a smoke. While strolling and smoking, we caught sight of one of the nuns from St. Goretti headed our way! I flicked my cigarette away but Kris wanted to finish hers, so she held it cupped in her hand and stuck her hand into her peacoat pocket.

"What are you doing off school grounds?" Sister demanded.

Well, we answered the only way we could in that situation. We lied through our teeth. By then, the cigarette had begun to burn Kris's palm and smoke was rising out of her coat pocket. The jig was *so* up! Kris and I could do nothing else but laugh.

We spent the next couple of days parked in the director of discipline's office listening to her anti-smoking diatribe. The discussion didn't work. I continued smoking until my college years, when I got fed up with paying seventy-five cents per pack.

Artistic Family

I never had much of a knack for artwork, so my mother helped me with my elementary-school projects. My fourth-grade teacher, Sr. Rose, knew I couldn't draw worth a lick so she was pretty sure Mom was helping me out. In fact, she once gave me two grades for a project: an A+ to my mother for artwork and a B+ to me for the written content.

When I reached the seventh grade, Sr. Rose became my science teacher. She assigned us a project to research eras of dinosaurs and to present our findings on poster boards. When I turned in my poster board, complete with colorful drawings, Sr. Rose noted the quality of

Mom's artwork.

"Mom didn't do it, Sister," I said. "My brother, Joey, did." Joey was in the fourth grade. Sister gave me an A+ for the project and the poster hung in her classroom for years. She never gave Joey a grade.

Snowball Fight

One of the many rules we had at our school was *never* throw snowballs on school property. Anyone caught hurling snow paid a fine (that was deposited into a mission fund), got paddled, and received a lecture about following rules. Nevertheless, my friends and I engaged in snowball fights on and off school property and were caught several times.

I always dreamed of clobbering a nun with a snowball and tried several times before finally hitting one in the back of the head. Sister saw me but never said a word. Several days later a group of us were heading home for lunch when we came upon the same nun, as well as several other sisters, standing on the sidewalk with their backs to us. After we passed by, one called my name. All of us turned in her direction and the nuns bombarded us with dozens of snowballs, laughing as they pelted us. I think they enjoyed the fight more than we did.

Snake Handler

My fourth-grade teacher showed us how tough nuns can be. We hid a garter snake in the middle desk drawer that she opened daily after lunch to retrieve her grade book. As we sat on the edge of our seats anticipating a scream, Sister reached into the drawer and pulled out the snake. "Okay, who does this belong to?" she calmly asked, waving the snake for us to see. I guess that prank backfired.

Bad Breath

Sister Clare had a mean case of bad breath. Eyes would water when she got up close and personal. For Christmas that year, all the boys chipped in and bought her a large bottle of Listerine. We attached a festive red bow to the bottle, set it on her desk, and fled. The next day she announced a thank-you to all of us boys for giving her such a nice present. She assured us she would share it with the other nuns. And we thought we had fooled Sr. Clare.

If You Can't Beat 'Em, Join 'Em

One Friday afternoon, in a hot and airless classroom stinking of tuna fish and peanut butter, Sr. Benedicta tried reading aloud to us from our literature book.

It was difficult to keep from nodding off, so we got into mischief. We did what we could to stay awake—whispering, passing notes, eating candy.

Abruptly, Sister Benedicta slammed the literature book on her desk. She directed us to line up at the door and not say a word. We obeyed. She led us down the stairs and told us to wait for a moment while she slipped into the gym. I just knew she was on the telephone calling our parents!

She rejoined our group and trooped us out of the building and into the dead-end street next to the school.

Sister Benedicta rolled up the sleeves of her habit and pulled out a bat and ball. "Play ball," she yelled. And we did!

I don't believe most nuns were ever given full credit for their insight and perception, but in one instance in 1955, I was among a small group of teenagers to encounter and appreciate the full breadth of one nun's wisdom.

Sisters and Shenanigans: Embarrassing Moments

Roaring Crabs

Sister Mary Thomas took extreme delight in me as I was teacher's pet. When I heard the laughter from a joke my older brother told my sister, I knew right off the bat Sr. Mary Thomas would enjoy listening to it. I asked Sister if she wanted to hear a joke.

"Yes, Teresa, go ahead."

"Why does the ocean roar?"

Not getting an answer from Sr. Mary Thomas, I continued, "Well, if you had crabs on your bottom, you would roar, too."

The expression on Sr. Mary Thomas's face never changed. I couldn't understand why she didn't laugh. That is, until a few years later, when I learned where our "bottoms" were, did I appreciate how humorless the joke must have been to her. It wasn't until decades later that I realized how both Sister and I totally missed the boat on that joke!

Brassy Hairdo

The London convent school I attended also served as a boarding school for teenage girls from Europe and South America. The girls came from so far to attend The Convent of the Sacred Heart of Mary because it was a superior finishing school and a safe place for them to learn English.

When I was fourteen years old, I was captivated by a Brazilian student's hair. She wore her auburn tresses long, hanging down her back in a single braid. Within that braid was a distinctive silver and gold stripe, beginning at her hairline and stretching to the tip of her braid. Quite exotic for 1954, I thought.

We other girls wondered if her streak was a natural gift from God, or was it a gift packaged in a dye bottle? If she did color it, then why didn't the nuns stop her, we mused? Intrigue, and even envy, struck us all. We all wanted streaks of our own but I was the only one stupid enough to try and create one.

I bought a bottle of peroxide and daubbed a little on my hair, which in those days I wore short and curly alá Gina Lollabrigida. Expecting to immediately see a silvery-gold shine, I ran to the mirror. Nothing happened. I daubbed a bit more. No luck. I daubed and daubed until half the bottle was gone. Still, no glamorous shimmering streak.

That evening I went to sleep disappointed but awoke to a bombshell the next morning. My hair had turned brassy blonde—but only half of it! The other part of my hair remained dark brown.

I faced a dire situation that morning as I walked into assembly sporting a pre-punk look that by even today's standards would be considered a bit daring. I can't recall the precise reactions of my peers and the nuns, but suffice it to say, I was ridiculed by the former and chastised by the latter.

One of the first things we learned about the nuns and their names was that we must address them as "Sister." "Yes, Sr. Joan" or even "Yes, Sister" was acceptable but never could we call them missus or ma'am. Never. Ever. Hell hath no fury like one of our nuns ma'amed. That really wasn't much of a problem for either of us since our parents were Yankee transplants where a "yes, Mom" or even a simple "yes" sufficed. Not so with our classmate, Robby. He was a boy whose Southern roots ran deep below the Mason-Dixon line. The rest of us ate Cream of Wheat for breakfast while Robby chowed down on grits (something neither one of us had ever seen, much less tasted, in our homes).

Most kids' first word is "mama," but we think Robby's was "ma'am." It was so ingrained in him that not a week went by when he didn't slip and ma'am Sister. Even attempts to correct himself didn't save him from Sister's ire.

Both of us live in the South, so we've added "yes, ma'am" and "no, ma'am" to our vocabularies and our children do the same. At times, it's been a challenge for us—but not anywhere near the uphill battle Robby faced trying to curb his nun-ma'aming habit.

M. P. and D. S.

Chapter Eight

A Sister by Any Other Name

"OKAY, SISTERS, LET'S TRY AND get it right this time. Scholastica, you begin."

"Yes, Mother. Sister Mark, would you like to light the candle?"

"Certainly, Mary Ellen, er, Sr. Mark," the nun answered. "Sister Jarlath, your turn," she said, trying to pass the lit taper to the nun.

Sister Jarlath didn't answer.

"Sister Jarlath? Sister Jarlath? *Margaret Pat!*" Sr. Mark yelled, sending Sr. Jarlath jumping to her feet.

"Oh, I'm so sorry," Sr. Jarlath said. "I just couldn't remember."

"Oh well, let's try it again," Mother John sighed. "You three are no longer Catherine, Mary Ellen, or Margaret Pat. You are Scholastica, Mark, and Jarlath," Mother Superior explained to the women who had just professed their religious vows.

As sisters, young girls broke ties to their previous lives. They moved from home and rarely saw or talked to family members. Probably the most daunting transition from miss to sister was changing their names. New monikers were not those heard in everyday Catholic settings such as Patricia and Kathleen. They most certainly were not the "Publics" names they envied, like Shirley or Debbie. Nuns were named after saints, deceased heroes of the Catholic faith living in heaven.

Saints occupy heavenly seats only after passing a rigid approval process that sometimes lasts hundreds of years. Becoming a saint meant a person had performed a heroic deed for his or her faith, like dying a torturous death. Saints-to-be were required to perform a couple of miracles, usually postmortem. It stands to reason naming sisters after saints would give the women role models to emulate. So, with more than 10,000 saints from which to choose, why then did so many girls select strange, often ancient and bizarre names like Evangelist or Crispin? Simple: Mother Superior made them.

A fact little known outside convent walls is that many orders' mother superiors selected names for their charges. Some mothers honored a nun-to-be's personal request, but others ignored petitions.

One former nun from Louisiana so deeply abhorred her name that fifty years later she still refused mentioning it to anyone, claiming it "horribly mannish." Mother Superior named her and other novices after area priests, all Cajuns whose names were most likely those common among bayou residents, such as Willis and Boudreaux.

Judging by how offbeat some names were, it seems many nuns might have been named the way Bluto nicknamed Delta fraternity pledges in *Animal House*. He gave recruits a quick once-over and dished out whatever popped into his mind, like "Flounder." There wasn't much recourse, either. If a young woman renamed Sr. Anthony questioned Mother Superior why that choice, she most likely was treated to a Bluto-like shrug of the shoulders. It's safe to assume Mother Superior stopped short of smashing a holy water cruet onto her forehead.

Perhaps names were meted out in a contest, a Holy Name Game that pitted naïve novices against Mother Superior. Flashing a Gene Rayburn grin, Mother Superior probably chatted with the girls to calm their pre-name jitters. Just like that television host, Reverend Mother might have started her own *Match Game* by tossing out clues:

"Ansillo."

"A form of penicillin?" Peggy answered.

"A Japanese monster movie?" said Claire.

"A seventh-century monk who became a saint with the feast day of October 11," Loretta chimed in.

"Ding, ding, ding, we've got a match," Mother Superior announced over the whooping and hollering of young novices celebrating Loretta's new name.

Although sisters most likely were assigned names of saints after whom they could model themselves, perhaps some were given names because they shared similar characteristics with a particular saint. A girl's appearance, attitude, or personality might have contributed to her chosen name. For example, a sweet, beautiful young thing unable to hold grudges might have been named after Saint Maria Goretti who, on her deathbed, forgave her rapist/murderer. An outspoken, passionate girl might have been named Sr. Joan de Arc while an athletic, energetic woman might have earned the name Sr. Sebastian, after the patron saint of athletes.

And if a young woman raised Mother Superior's ire? She could have been saddled with Willibrod, Angscar, or Polycarp.

"Mother Prioress (Superior) must have liked me," Rosemary, a former nun recalled. "Otherwise, she would have given me a name like Eusebius or Philomena the way she did the other novices, instead of Mary Grace."

Not just any Saint Tom, Dick, or Harry would do. Suspicion has it mother superiors relied on a secret list before selecting names. For starters, most male saints, and female saints who were virgin martyrs, gained automatic approval. Some of the Johnny-come-latelys like Native American Kateri Tekakwitha were probably at the bottom of the list. In fact, Tekakwitha technically has not reached sainthood (she is "Blessed") but she and others may only have been added to the list in a move toward creating cultural diversity in the convent. Chinese saint Martha Wang and St. Moses the Black from Ethiopia probably also vied for those politically correct slots.

Assigning men's names was extremely popular. Taking on a man's name and going from Alice to Thomas, without undergoing an operation, had to have been the ultimate test of obedience and piety.

Once they shook off rumors that only ugly nuns were named after men, with a little practice, sisters grew accustomed to calling each other names like Luke and Paul.

Students often figured out what kind of teacher they were facing, just by her name. Sisters named after a tortured saint were usually the crankiest, especially if their namesakes died on the rack or were beheaded. And if their namesakes were boiled in oil like Saint Barbara, kids started their days with novenas to St. Jude, patron saint of lost causes.

Sister Joseph of Cupertino's students knew their mischief-making days were over. Legend recalls St. Joseph levitated and whipped himself around the church, sailing over congregants' heads and flying from corner to corner. Any nun named for the "flying friar" most certainly would share his knack for being everywhere at once.

SISTER WHO?

Idealistic novices yearned for spiritual role models with beautiful, easy-on-the-ears names. Mother superiors often selected from one of those on the sisters' most desired list but they also chose from their own favorites. Number one on both lists, though, was Mary. Many orders even required using Mary along with another name, like Sr. Mary Patrick. When you're the mother of God *and* a virgin, it's tough not to make the top of any nun's list.

The most sought-after names by nuns-in-the-making probably included these:

Bernadette—Always a favorite saint, Bernadette's popularity soared after *The Song of Bernadette* took home four Oscars at the 1943 Academy Awards.

Rose—St. Rose of Lima loved tending her garden: planting seeds and watching them grow into beautiful flowers. Her nurturing nature was an ideal match for sisters headed to the classroom.

Therese—Sisters named after "The Little Flower" hoped to evoke her image of a quiet sufferer.

Lucy—Rough-and-tumble girls were keen on St. Lucy, who tore out her eyes and gave them to a suitor she didn't like.

Clare—As television took hold during the mid-twentieth century, it only seemed natural that its patron saint be chosen by girls who grew up in front of the tube.

Catherine—Any girl who could tell a pope what to do (and he did it!) would be the perfect namesake for strong-willed, opinionated novices.

Anne—Mother of the virgin who gave birth to God? 'Nuff said.

Mother Superiors' lists probably looked like this:

Agatha—Virgin and martyr
Agnes—Virgin and martyr
Dymphna—Virgin and martyr
Benedicta—Virgin and martyr
Philomena—Virgin and martyr
Gregory, Hubert, Ambrose, Boniface, Bonaventure, and any other male saint, martyred or not. Virginity didn't play into the choice, either, as not much is noted about the chastity of male saints.

Stepping into a classroom and discovering your teacher was a Sr. Adrian or Sr. Lawrence sent more children home crying for their mamas than did a Saturday afternoon watching the creature climb out of the Black Lagoon. Saint Adrian, the patron saint of butchers, died by being torn limb from limb. Saint Lawrence was tortured on a hot griddle, purportedly yelling to his captors he was done on one side and needed turning. Kids really looked forward to being stuck in a class where each day meant risking being torn to bits or placed on a hot seat.

By the 1960s, the outside world was slowly breaking through convent walls and most mother superiors recognized certain names could bring turmoil into the classroom. Tuning into *The Ed Sullivan Show* would have given them the good sense to retire certain saints from the list. What kind of respect could a sister expect if she were named after Saints Englebert, Fabian, or Liberatus? At least there was no St. Elvis.

The wisest of mother superiors turned to children when determining the suitability of a nun's name. She envisioned the reaction forty thirteen-year-olds might have to particular names. Under that criterion, she wouldn't hesitate to scratch St. Lawdog off the list. After considering saints Homobonus and Fulk, Mother Superior ripped their pages out of her saints' directory, set them on fire, and threw the ashes into the incense burner.

Not long after sisters received new names came nicknames. How could a nun expect otherwise? As difficult and strange some of the names must have sounded to the sisters, they set off an imagination explosion in the minds of ten-year-olds. Most began as silly abbreviations, such as Big V for Veronica or Sr. Claude for Claudette. Others focused on physical features.

"One of our nuns was a large woman. She wasn't fat, just squarely built," said Stephanie (Sellers) Mazzon. "We called her Sister Truck. Behind her back, of course."

Gayle Hogwood recalls a nickname she and her friends gave a nun just because the sister was ill.

"Sister Dorothea, who wore a brown habit, suffered from allergies one Christmas season. Her nose was bright red. All we could see was the red nose in a sea of brown. We called her 'Sr. Dottie, the red-nosed-reindeer.'

"Behind her back, of course."

Other nicknames evolved simply because it was the natural thing to do. One woman recalls nuns named Sr. Oliver and Sr. Martine. To their students, they were Martini and the Olive. Behind their backs, of course.

Bestselling author Mary Higgins Clark came clean in her memoir

Kitchen Privileges. All the nuns were formally called "Mother"—Mother Superior, Mother St. Margaret, Mother St. Thomas, and Mother St. Patrick.

"They became known more familiarly among us as Soupy, Maggie, Tommie, and Patty."

Behind their backs, of course.

Some pet names came as a result of playground one-upmanship over kids from public school. It was easy enough to shrug off "old lady Henderson's" bad breath but when Publics started bragging about Miss Smith's shapely legs, Catholic children revolted. They hatched legends like "Hippo Hugo" hiding a herd of children under her habit and tales describing "Cole Slaw Stanislaus" shaving her head every night.

A few nuns were their own undoing when it came to nicknames. Katy Doyle reported that one young nun's great rapport with her students eventually led to her moniker. Sister Mary Elizabeth started each day telling elephant jokes. She soon became known as Sister Mary Elephant, Doyle said, adding that it was good Sister was slim or the name-calling could have landed them in hot water.

Sister Drusilla's superhero persona earned her not only a pet name but also a song created in her honor.

"Sister Drusilla was a sight to behold," Diana Leonard said. "She liked to toss her elbow-length veil over her shoulders, like a cape. She'd stand sentry in the hallway, cape flipped back and hands planted firmly on her hips."

"She transformed into 'Mighty Moose,' whose sole purpose was restoring noisy halls to their rightful states of silence," Leonard recalled. In Leonard's all-girl school, it was nearly impossible to maintain total silence. As the girls grew louder, Sr. Mighty Moose quickened her stride, pacing up and down the hallways until the din grew unbearable. Leonard said Sister would then stand still and bellow:

"You, in the plaid skirt. Stop immediately."

Hallway traffic skidded to a halt. No one knew who she was yelling at because everyone wore identical plaid uniforms. Then, like Superman, Sister flew up and down the hallway, her cape nearly airborne as she tried identifing the talkers. Leonard and her friends were so impressed by Sister's alter ego that they created "Mighty Moose," a ditty sung to the tune of the *Mickey Mouse Club Show* theme song.

Just when baby boomers were learning it was normal to call a woman Michael or Dominic came The Change. Thanks to the Vatican II Council, sisters were given the opportunity to revert back to their baptismal names. Quicker than they could utter "Saints preserve us," sisters queued up to reclaim original names. Good-bye Sister Mary Stephen, hello Sister Laura.

Not only were Catholics trying to adjust to seeing nuns with legs and arms, now they were faced with learning to call them by different names. Real names, too, just like those of their mothers and grandmothers. For the first time, kids (and many parents) realized nuns were not only human, but women. Another divine mystery had been disclosed.

Vatican II threw millions of students into a quandary. Which name were they to call Sister? Do we use her saint name or her new/old name, children worried. Most went along with the changes and called sisters by their birth names, figuring that to be the wiser option. A Sr. Andrea might less likely pack a wallop than a nun named after St. George, the dragon slayer. A few tried playing it safe, calling nuns by both names. As difficult as it was to call up their new names, it was doubly hard to remember nuns whose birth names were actually names of saints: Sr. Aloysius became Sr. Jane but Sr. Jane became Sr. Ann. Confusion reigned!

The most disturbing part of the name change was that it obliterated a generations-old system for identifying cantankerous nuns. Before Vatican II, a Sr. Mary Patricia would have earned a green light: clear sailing ahead. The light turned amber for nuns with male names, like a Sister Anthony. Kids proceeded with caution. Those nuns who dropped the saint's first name and were called only by a last name like Sr. Borromeo (instead of Sr. Charles Borromeo), earned a red light warning. All frivolity hit a dead end. With names like Sister Beth or

Sister Colleen, however, it was virtually impossible for students to grasp how much trouble they were in until a hand rested on the scruff of the neck or an eraser clipped an ear.

It really didn't matter what names sisters were called. A sister by any other name was still a sister. Although he wasn't talking about nuns, President Kennedy said it all: "Forgive your enemies, but never forget their names."

One truth remained absolute, however. Even if Sister now went by the name of Betsy, no one dared to call her Miss Betsy.

WHAT'S IN A NAME?

Technically, there is a difference between a "nun" and a "sister." A nun lives in a cloistered religious community and has professed solemn vows of poverty, chastity, and obedience. Nuns are restricted from leaving their cloister, and their work is done within the confines of their convent or monastery. A sister is not cloistered and has professed simple vows of poverty, chastity, and obedience. A sister's work is done outside the convent. To the general public, though, the term is interchangeable and both are called "Sister."

I was serving Mass with three other seventh graders, Patrick, Louis, and Richard. We were old pros and knew exactly what to do on the altar. Experience, however, gave way to cockiness. Nothing went right. Patrick knocked over the bells. Louis stepped on the back of Richard's cassock, sending a ripping sound throughout the sanctuary, and Richard spilled water from the finger bowl. Reverence, already in short supply in middle school, gave way to laughter.

Celebrating Mass was Father O'Shea, a serious guy who had a gnat's sense of humor. Since I was vice-president of the altar boy society and would receive the most grief for screw-ups, I whispered admonishments after each snafu.

During the processional to the back of the church after Mass, Fr. O'Shea berated us the entire way. When we reached the sacristy, Father yelled at me: "Mike Prendergast, you were the worst one." Just then, Sr. Bertha walked in and heard Father's diatribe.

Sister gazed into our faces with a twisted, maniacal stare that I only saw one other time in my life, many years later, on boxer Mike Tyson's face just seconds before he bit off Evander Holyfield's ear. She demanded to know more. Father detailed our immature, distracting, and irreverent behavior. "Someone even *talked* during the consecration," he said. He was referring to me. I had told the guys to knock it off. Murdering the pope was considered a less serious offense than speaking during the consecration. I was ready to die.

She demanded the culprit's identity. Father O'Shea shot a look in my direction but then told Sister to forget it. At first, I wondered why Father O'Shea didn't turn me in. Then I recalled his glance. He had the look of a man who, as a child, might have faced a nun in a similar situation—maybe for even talking during the consecration. Perhaps this memory triggered Father's rare fit of forgiveness.

Much like Father O'Shea's, my own memories of nuns affect my behavior today. I kneel straight up in church, never letting my butt hit the pew. I genuflect, without thinking, every time I enter or leave a pew. When asked to volunteer at a homeless shelter, I remember the sisters' drill: "Whatsover you do for the least of my brothers, that you do unto me." But most importantly, if Osama Bin Laden himself were to walk up to me during Mass and leave a lumpy backpack, I would never even *think* of talking during the consecration.

M. P.

Chapter Nine

A Legacy:
Cheeky Girls and
Worthless Boys Grow Up

SISTER CLARE FACED A SEA of faces awash in smiles, all beaming in anticipation of the day's events. After twelve long years, the graduating class of 1968 was about to leave St. Basil's protective confines. Good-bye uniforms, good-bye rules, and good-bye Sister. But shaking loose from Sr. Clare wasn't as easy as walking out the door.

Sister had years of service invested in these kids. She tackled the tough job of fashioning unruly children into morally unscathed young adults ready to take on the world. Sister taught them how to make the sign of the cross, to genuflect, and to stand when Father Donohue walked into the room. She spent hours drilling them on the *Baltimore Catechism*, helping them memorize prayers, and walking them through countless rosary processions. Sister Clare guided them through adolescent temptations and comforted them when sorrow broke their hearts. Now, she spoke her final words:

"Remember, what you are is God's gift to you. What you make of yourself is your gift to God."

The students bolted out of the schoolyard and on to college, war, jobs, marriage, families, and life away from St. Basil's. Wherever they went, though, Sr. Clare followed. That's the way it was with Catholic nuns. No one could shake off a sister's influence.

By the late 1960s, nuns like Sr. Clare ruled the Catholic landscape. Well, at least the parish school. Some lumbered up and down hallways, the pounding of sensible shoes warning their arrival. Others soared, robes flying and wings outstretched as they hovered overhead, protecting their young from preying wildlife. Their presence was formidable—and ebbing.

Just like their prehistoric counterparts', the rule of dogma's dinosaurs ended abruptly. Catholic schools teemed with dozens of shrouded women and, nearly overnight, most disappeared from the classrooms. Their reign may have ended but not their clout. Much like their ancient predecessors, nuns inspired awe, respect, and fear during their heyday while creating impressions that would last a millennium.

Larger than life, a nun commanded immediate attention and reverence from her students, often in ways that could never be erased from a child's memory. Just her stepping into a room was enough for children to take heed of Sister, mostly out of admiration but sometimes from raw terror. A sister bellowing "You, young man," cleared hallways faster than the class sexpot screaming, "Spin the bottle out back in ten minutes!" Boys scrambled in all directions, whether guilty of wrongdoing or not. Sticking around to argue with Sister was useless. Even hulking adolescents who wouldn't pass up a schoolyard scrap shriveled under a nun's scowl.

As easily as some children—and adults—feared being around a nun, just being in Sister's presence honored others. Maybe do-gooders hoped nunly holiness would rub off on them, or perhaps they saw it as a *mea culpa* for a momentary slip. Imagine, a child ends his nightly prayer requesting a tornado strike the convent sometime before the next day's math test. Morning dawns, bringing clear skies and a repentant urge to lug Sister's books.

Desire for sisters' attention often intensified as children got older. Offers to rake the convent yard, organize the cloakroom, or sort out Sister's hankie drawer poured in. Adulthood rarely diminished yearnings for sisterly affection. Elderly women broke out into heated arguments during Friday night bingo over whose turn it was to scrub the convent floor. Shuttling nuns around town in the family station wagon, though, was *the* pinnacle of piety in a parish. Drivers sailed the streets, tossing a holier-than-thou wave to women lower on the let's-get-in-Sister's-good-graces pecking order—those stuck mimeographing tests and handling other classroom scutwork.

Karen (Alsback) Johnson recalls her grandmother's penchant for chauffeuring nuns around Lindherst, New Jersey, in a beat-up Ford Fairlane. Johnson said watching her tiny grandmother, who could barely see over the steering wheel, cruise around town with a pack of black-shrouded nuns in tow was a comical sight. She also suspects her grandmother had a motive beyond lending a helping hand.

"She never said it, but I think she believed she would enter heaven sooner by driving the nuns to and fro," Johnson said. "She deserved early admission. Those nuns were bossy!"

A nun's influence over her students didn't end just because they were no longer in her classroom. Nuns managed to hold an upper hand over their students long after the children left school. Bumping into two fully habited sisters pushing shopping carts in Wal-Mart decades after most nuns had given up the traditional garb hurtled one man back in time like Dr. Who. No longer was he a middle-aged businessman shopping for office supplies but a gawky ten-year-old barreling through hallways after the tardy bell had rung. The encounter drew a schoolboy politeness out of him, along with a pinch of wariness. Before "Good morning, Sisters," rolled off his tongue, the man had buried his hands deep into his pockets.

Sisters did more than instruct children, which might explain their long-felt presence. They crafted moral frameworks, teaching children life lessons that would help them form values to carry into adulthood. Sometimes, these lessons were part of the curriculum and found in schoolbooks. Reading texts featuring John and Jean, the Catholic version of Dick and Jane, were packed with examples of kindness. Other times, sisters relied on sharing saint stories to teach courage, bravery, and good decision-making.

Many times, lessons were uncomplicated and not found in school-books or stories. A gentle squeeze from Sister's hand demonstrated kind-heartedness in a way no book or lesson plan could. An unspoken bond between a sister and a young boy could mark a soft spot in his heart that remained tender forty years later.

"I was a typical redhead boy, rambunctious and full of energy. The sisters had a tough time with me in first and second grade," Bill Walsh said. "To tell the truth, I really didn't enjoy school, or the nuns. That all changed in third grade."

A kind and supportive woman, Sr. Elizabeth Rose took Walsh under her wing. Her eyes twinkled, her voice resonated warmth and kindness, Walsh remembers. "Third grade was a great year for me. I even earned a spot on the honor roll."

"Sister Elizabeth Rose and I had a connection, some sort of bond. It wasn't until a few years later that I discovered exactly how we were linked."

It was post-Vatican II and the nuns' habits changed, exposing limbs and hair for the first time. As Walsh gawked at the strange new sight, Sr. Mary Rose breezed alongside him, her eyes glowing and her mouth turned up in a grin. Immediately, he recognized their connection.

"Just like me, flaming red curls covered Sister's head."

Sisters reinforced these life lessons with "nunisms," pithy advice they threw out in frustration or when they had just emerged from thirty minutes' meditation and were in a reflective mood. Some made no sense to the students, like Sr. Maximilian's advice to a class clown: "Steve Cronin, you are a fool. Fools are cheap around here." Where were fools expensive, children wondered?

Other sayings might have been confusing to a young child, but became clear later in life, such as one girl's note from Sister: "Life's path is white as the driven snow. Be careful how you tread it, for every mark will show."

For Cynthia Kellerman, Sister's words echo in her head today, reminding her to enjoy life.

Sister faced her students each morning with a huge smile and twinkling eyes, and began class by proclaiming, "Laughter is the fore-taste of heaven," Kellerman recalled. To this day, Kellerman says she envisions the nun's cheery face framed in her Sisters of Charity bonnet. Because of that memory, Kellerman savors every good laugh she can get as a gift from God—or from a sister.

Not all nunisms were positive. One man recalls being told in the third grade how worthless he would always be because he was left-handed. The young boy didn't take Sister's words to heart as he went on to graduate Phi Beta Kappa from law school and became a successful trial lawyer.

Some nuns applied reverse psychology, hoping their words would not be forgotten and would instead light a fire under potential under-achievers. Jerry Barthelemy chuckles today over Sr. Anthony's advice to him years ago.

"Sister told me I wouldn't make a good garbage collector, much less anything else. I never forgot her words," Barthelemy said. "When I graduated from college, I sent her one of my announcements so she could see how well I did for myself." Sister sent a note back to him, explaining she often played down students' abilities so they might be motivated to do better and prove her wrong.

Sister closed her note with a zinger, though. "Will you be seeking employment in the supervision of the local garbage collection union? Ha Ha! Gotcha!"

Nuns often served as anchors in stormy times, their compassion grabbing firmly on to a little one's heart and remaining there for a lifetime. Meredith Walker was eleven years old and the eldest of four children when her mother died of cancer. Her father, overwrought with grief, grew numb to his children's needs. The nuns from her school stepped in, coming to her home and helping care for them as well as providing spiritual support. In return, her dad developed a lifelong friendship with those sisters, even sitting bedside to one of the nuns when she died years later.

Even though many folks tell of receiving life-altering inspiration from the nuns, most people admit a subtler imprint. Most common-ly, sisters helped children forge good habits and routines they hoped would last throughout their lives. One mother reported ushering her young children into church pews with the snap of her fingers, a signal for them to drop to one knee in genuflection. The move was a reflex triggered from years of reacting to *the click, click, click* of a nun's metal clicker, she said.

Remnants of the sisters' love of order, routine, and flair for processions can be found in all walks of life today. A woman visiting her elderly mother in a Catholic-run nursing home chuckled over the influence nuns must have had over staff orderlies.

"Outside the dining hall, a row of wheelchairs lined the hallway, one parked behind another making a straight line. It looked just the way we children were lined up to move in between classes," Marjorie Ringstrom said.

Nuns crafted more than lasting impressions. Many were beacons, illuminating a path leading to adult livelihoods. Of course, religious life was the number one vocation they tried steering children toward. Sisters were too clever to ram the message down kids' throats, knowing that if asked, most children would sooner sign up as tasters at a spinach farm than join them in a religious order.

More than one sister knew a young girl's weak spot: romance. Many sisters shared details of a glorious "wedding day" and glowed when they described their white gowns. Sisters flashed silver wedding bands and dreamily referred to themselves as "brides of Christ." Little girls in parishes nationwide tied rosary beads to their waistbands, tossed towels over their heads in veil-like fashion, and insisted on being called Sr. Patty or Sr. Nancy. The really enamored ones took on their fathers' names like Sr. Malcolm or Sr. Francis.

At one parish, sisters encouraged older girls to consider devoting their adult lives to Christ by joining an order (preferably theirs) of nuns. Sister enticed them with a tour of the convent, allowing them to visit one of the nun's bedrooms, Liz McManus remembers.

"Even though most of us girls thought 'no way,' we never considered it strange or weird that women chose the lives they led. It just wasn't for us."

Boys weren't left out of religious recruitment, either. Mike Brownlee recalls playing priest and making his own communion hosts by cutting circles in Dandee bread with bottle caps. He and his buddies preferred Necco candies, thin fruit-flavored wafers. Father Mike solemnly went down the row of kneeling boys and girls, praying *Corpus Christi* before placing a lemon or cherry Jesus on the waiting tongue. Naturally, little Sr. Malcolm stood behind communicants waiting to see if they chewed or not. Brownlee admitted that even though boys pretended being priests, they really wanted to be nuns. That way, they could hold the pointer and be the whacker instead of the whackee, he explained.

Eventually most children sought out different careers, many the result of a nun's influence. Whether due to wise words or the carryover of behavior instilled in them, children took on responsibilities and jobs reflective of their years under a nun's supervision. Sometimes, specific childhood duties led to life callings. For Anna Samuels, her daily housecleaning duties took on meaning and purpose, advancing her toward a career as a school custodian. It was an honorable job, and one she took on with resolve learned years ago from the nuns.

Sisters sometimes unintentionally introduced careers to children. Maggie Hawkins, a product of Canadian nuns during the early 1970s, theorized why children in later decades were whacked on hands with long, rubber-tipped pointers instead of the stereotypical ruler used in previous years.

"Somewhere in a nun's classroom sat a boy watching a tiny sister standing on her tiptoes using a ruler to point out Greenland on a map hanging from the top of the chalkboard," Hawkins said. "Noticing how the nun couldn't reach the top of the map with her ruler, and feeling a civic duty that generations not grow up thinking Greenland was located in Ireland, the boy went on to invent a longer tool diminutive nuns could use—the pointer."

He sold millions of them to the Catholic-school system, long overstaffed by short nuns, she continued with her theory. "Sisters were probably busy pointing out lessons when we got out of line and smacked us with whatever was handier, first a ruler and then, later, the pointer," she said.

Once students moved beyond religious vocations, they often chose careers reminding them of nuns. A sister's propensity to set down rules and make sure everyone followed them, along with her preference for black-and-white clothing, led children toward careers as police officers, judges, and basketball referees.

Although most sisters' protégés led productive lives working jobs and raising families, many of their young wards have gone on to positions of prestige, fame, and sometimes, fortune. Actor Danny DeVito, NBC correspondent Tim Russert, author Nora Roberts, and television superstar Oprah Winfrey have all acknowledged the influence Catholic nuns have had on their lives. Devito credits nuns for his biting wit, Roberts her sense of discipline, and Russert his introduction to journalism. Winfrey's gift-giving pilgrimage to Africa in 2003 was inspired, in part, by nuns who brought food and gifts to her home Christmas day when she was twelve years old.

Ultimately, sisters' legacy may simply be the stories they generated. Most tales are humorous, innocent reminders of an era long past. Routines like tossing a ball at recess or ordering a school lunch take on a twist when they're recalled with an anecdote about Sister Alfred or Sister Mary Agnes. Points of inspiration, admiration, wonderment, love, and even fear, these recollections are pieces of a heritage passed from one generation to the next.

MEMORIES OF SISTERS' INFLUENCE

Sister's Gift: A Lasting First Impression

The Doctor

I didn't really know what kind of medical care my sister had received because so many of her fifty years as a nun were cloistered. Cecelia had always been a very healthy woman, though, and I suspected she might never have gone to a doctor. My husband and I urged her to visit a doctor when serious symptoms plagued her. She finally relented. It was not good. Cecelia was diagnosed with a critical condition.

Even though my sister became seriously ill with a tumor, her faith in God remained steadfast. She assured us that nothing terrible would happen to her. Cecelia was realistic about her prognosis yet sincere in her efforts to try other routes of healing. When the treatments didn't work, and she turned sicker and sicker, Cecelia's doctor convinced her to have the tumor removed.

Following Cecelia's surgery, her doctor, a handsome middle-aged man resembling Arthur Ashe, discussed the outcome with us. He was optimistic about the surgery's success yet warned that the presence of even one cell could mean she might still have cancer. At that point, he advised us all we could do was pray. Then he slipped into Cecelia's room to carry on the discussion with her.

For the next five days the surgeon continued to visit my sister, sometimes spending as much as forty-five minutes to an hour with her. On her final day in the hospital, we thanked the doctor for his kindness in spending so much time with Cecelia, especially considering his busy schedule.

"Oh, you've got no reason to thank *me*," the doctor said. "These precious moments with Sr. Cecelia have been incredibly meaningful and rewarding.

"Sister Cecelia has given me spiritually far more than anything I could have given her."

That kind doctor passed away two years later. My sister, now ninety and seven years past her illness, is still with us.

There Go I

Sister Marguerite caught me being catty, rudely talking about another girl. She grabbed me by the back of my shirt and dragged me into the girls' bathroom, where she shoved me toward the mirror.

"Look in the mirror and say 'There but for the Grace of God go I.'"

Her words struck hard. I could have been in that girl's shoes. Years later, I passed that phrase on to my kids and my students.

Dove Sighting

I had just delivered a load of donated food and supplies to the Carmelite nuns cloistered in their convent not too far from my home and had driven through a severe thunderstorm to get there. The convent was located in an area that flooded easily, but as we neared the grounds the rain stopped. We unloaded all the groceries, and as we were leaving the convent sunshine broke through the clouds. When we got closer to the van, I spotted a white dove perched on the roof. Only at a convent, I thought, and awe inspiring, to say the least.

The Sisters and Me

When our very large Catholic family of twelve moved into our new home, we discovered our house shared a common fence with Blessed Sacrament Church and school grounds. Our father broke through the fence and installed a gate. We were the only students who could walk out their back gate and be at school.

Living so close to the school, I got to know the nuns outside the classroom. Some of the sisters were so stern that I nicknamed them the Sisters of the Holy Order of Iron Shorts. It was a mystery to me how the nuns could teach us about a loving, nurturing, and forgiving God but use force to do so.

Recycling Shoes and Spirits

Sister Aquinas never threw anything away and was adamant that we never did either. Instead, we saved and collected our recyclables for area migrant farm workers.

About a dozen of us women at St. Juliana's, an upper-middle-class parish in West Palm Beach, Florida, regularly tended to a church garden. To avoid ruining our shoes and sandals in the muck, we kicked them off in a pile in the church's social hall and then walked barefoot to the garden.

We returned a little while later only to find our shoes missing. The culprit was a mystery, but, as in most Catholic parishes, eighth-grade boys were immediate suspects.

Not this time. Sr. Aquinas saw our shoes piled on the floor, mistook them for trash, and carted them off to a migrant camp in the western reaches of the county. The following week, in the middle of the winter vegetable capital of the world, women of all ages trudged up and down rows of lettuce, tomatoes, and bell peppers sporting chic Cole Haans, Papagallos, and Ferragamos.

Sister Aquinas was a remarkable woman. Her vocal cords had been damaged in a surgery and she could talk only in a whisper. When she spoke, however, she grabbed the attention of everyone in a room, including that of us shoeless women.

The tireless work of Sr. Aquinas, who is often remembered as the Mother Teresa of the Palm Beaches, helped lift the standard of living and spirit of so many of God's children she served.

Mistaken Identity

My children attended a preschool run by a local Christian church. The church was producing the musical *The Sound of Music* and organizers planned to offer a preview to guests attending the school's annual grandparents' day.

I brought my mom and dad for grandparents' day, and as we entered the school's foyer, we were greeted by a swarm of chorus members dressed in costumes—nuns' habits.

"Oh my goodness, you have nuns at this school! How wonderful," my father gushed.

I really hated breaking the news to him that the women weren't nuns, just actors.

Sister's Gift: A Shove in the Right Direction

Cleaning Career

I entered Good Shepherd Orphanage as an abandoned five-year-old in the late 1940s and lived there until adulthood. The home was a grand old castle. Living there was an adventure.

Since the orphanage was my home, the nuns gave me household

duties. The home was four stories tall and filled with banquet-sized rooms and oversized floors. One of my jobs was to wax and polish the floors. We girls strapped cleaning rags to our shoes and waltzed, back and forth, back and forth, until the floors shined.

Another one of my chores was cleaning the windows—on all four floors! On the upper levels, I hung out the window with my feet tucked under the bed rail as my only safeguard from falling.

All these chores have served me well. For more than ten years, I've been the sole custodian at a school with grades kindergarten through twelfth. I do a good job, too.

Heavenly Elephants

Our days at St. Margaret's began at 8:30 A.M. Mass. All eight classes with fifty to sixty kids in each filled the church. I guess we were a bit rowdy, because Sister Lucy could only shake her head at us and say, "It is more likely for an elephant to squeeze through a peephole than for you to graduate from St. Margaret's."

Special Guidance

My grades were very good my freshman year of high school but I signed up for the easiest subjects I could take for my sophomore year, including woodworking and commercial arithmetic (instead of geometry). My interest at that time was to quit school when I turned sixteen and get a job.

Sister Mary Angele, my homeroom teacher, read my schedule and called me in for a career chat. She told me that I was too good of a student to be taking such easy courses. Sister Mary Angele urged me to change directions. She gained permission for me to take, at the same time, advanced algebra and geometry. In 1944, I graduated the top math student in my class of more than 300 students and received a special medal. I also decided to go on to college, becoming the first person in my family to do so.

I studied engineering at Purdue University and went on to receive high honors and an invitation to join the top honorary society for engineering students, Tau Beta Pi. After graduating with an engineering degree, I pursued a career lasting more than forty years. My final position was president of a computer systems company in 1990.

To think, I nearly dropped out of high school. I will be forever thankful to Sister Mary Angele for what she did for me.

Works for Me

As an elementary-school teacher, my memories of school with the nuns are very dear. I even find myself injecting a little fear and guilt into my lessons about values.

Whispering Hope

I attended public school for my first four years and preferred athletics to academics, which often led to my getting into trouble. I could never pass up a fight. I transferred to Catholic school in fifth grade but I still showed no interest in my studies. I was even held back that year.

My young life changed when I entered the eighth grade and encountered Sister Serphine. She showered me with special interest and worked hard to help keep me going in my studies. Sister taught me I could still take part in sports and succeed in school.

Lab Rat

I was not a very good math student. I hated geometry and midway through the school year found myself failing. Sister Benedicta suggested I come to her classroom after dismissal for tutoring.

When I arrived, she told me to close and lock the door. Of course, I did as I was told but also wondered if this would be my last day on Earth. Sister instructed me to sit in the chair next to her desk.

"Jerome, there is no way you are going to pass my class at the rate you are going. No matter how many hours of extra work we do here, you still won't pass," she said, leaning back in her chair.

"Therefore, if you help me with a special project, and don't tell anyone, I promise you will pass my class." My seedy brain conjured all kinds of possibilities for what she wanted me to do, especially since the door behind me was locked.

Sister Benedicta led me into the room next door, our biology and chemistry lab. A vat containing a variety of creatures awaiting dissection sat on the table. She handed me a large bullfrog and asked if I could dissect it for her. I loved that aspect of biology, which I had studied the previous year. My biology teacher told Sister I had been one of the better lab students. Sister also knew that I currently was enrolled in a correspondence course in taxidermy.

Three nights a week, Sister had been attending college to complete her bachelor's degree. With teaching a full day at school and attending classes at night, along with all her religious responsibilities, Sister couldn't find time for the dissection projects in her biology class. We struck a deal. Over the next several months I spent at least one day a week in the lab after school dissecting Sister's specimens. She continually reminded me to remain silent about our arrangement, which I did. In return, I passed her class. Others wondered how my grades jumped from failing to passing but I never told anyone, not even my parents.

Several years later, I was writing a class newsletter article about some of our former nuns and I contacted Sister Benedicta by telephone. She told me she couldn't place my name with a face. I asked her, "What grades did you get in your college biology class? You never told me."

"Dang, this has to be Jerome."

Sister Irma's Pitch

I write for a living because of what Sr. Mary Irma, O.S.U., taught me in 1962 during my final semester in fifth grade at St. Jerome School in Cleveland, Ohio. She taught me that writing pays off. She illustrated the point with the most prized payoff any Cleveland fifth grader and Little Leaguer could possibly imagine: tickets to a Cleveland Indians twi-night doubleheader.

Back in those days, the Cleveland Press awarded baseball tickets to any kid who managed to get a straight-A report card. A powerful motivator if we played by the rules, but Sister Irma knew that in my case the goal was well out of reach. I had three strikes against me: geography, arithmetic, and science.

Fortunately for me, Sister made her own rules. She cut me a deal. If I wrote ten essays, she'd give me A's across the board. Now, that nun could pitch! But if she could spot my weakness, I could spot hers. My first essay was titled: "My Future Career as a Priest."

I scribbled the other nine essays in short order. Several weeks remained before the end of the term, so she upped the ante. By the final bell, I had given her twenty-five essays. She made good on her promise.

I took my dad to the twi-nighter in August. I'll never forget that perfect summer night. That was one of my final memories of him; he suffered a stroke and died before the end of the season.

Sister Irma is gone now, too, but my gratitude remains for the precious gift she gave me. It occurs to me that I should express my thanks to her in a way she would appreciate.

So here it is, Sister. One more essay.

Sister's Gift: Lifetime Memories of Dedication, Influence, and Respect

Worldly News

In her late seventies and in her final year of teaching, Sr. Mary Ambrose had been given leeway to educate us pretty much any way she desired. This was good news for her and even greater news for us, her sixth-grade students.

For forty years, Sister had fussed over using textbooks she considered inadequate. At long last, her superiors relented and instructed her to do as she pleased. What pleased her was obtaining subscriptions to the *Wall Street Journal* and *The New York Times* for the eight of us in her class.

Using those newspapers in lieu of textbooks, Sr. Mary Ambrose created the most intellectually exciting experience of my young life. Sister brought the world to our classroom. Although she was afflicted by the frailty of old age, Sister's enthusiasm never waned. Each day she encouraged us to work hard—the world was at our doorstep. Even as youngsters, we recognized the respect Sr. Mary Ambrose drew from those around her. We children were in awe. Apparently, so were her fellow nuns. In addition to giving Sister free reign over her students, the other nuns relocated Sr. Mary Ambrose's personal room right next door to the classroom so that she could slip away and rest for a moment when fatigue overcame her.

Sister Mary Ambrose's attitude toward education was bold and truly *avant garde* for the 1930s. She was a woman ahead of her time. For that, I am always grateful.

Storytelling Sister

Sister Alphonse, a dear friend of mine for more than thirty years, was noted for her storytelling. We hung on her every word. Sister's friends have grown to appreciate her gift even more now that she suffers from Alzheimer's disease.

Her personal conversion to Catholicism was one of Sr. Alphonse's more popular stories. It seems her mother was a Kennedy (not one of *those* Kennedys) who married a firefighter named Katz. We weren't sure, but gathered from her that since her mother was not a practicing Catholic, and because of her father's last name and indifference to Catholicism, Sister believed her father might have been Jewish. Whatever the facts, there was no churchgoing in her household.

When Sr. Alphonse was a first grader, she latched on to another little girl who shared with her details of a mystical, wonderful place she visited every Sunday. It was St. Patrick's Cathedral. To Sr. Alphonse, it was a castle draped in majestic finery hidden behind great iron doors. Sister Alphonse longed to pass through those gates and experience the splendor for herself. Her chance to do exactly that came through an invitation from her little friend.

Sister Alphonse noticed her friend never visited the great building without wearing a blue beret on top of her head. Not wanting to enter the magic building looking differently than the other girl, Sr. Alphonse saved her pennies and bought her own beret at the five-and-dime. The one-day excursion turned into a lifetime vocation.

A few years after her first visit to St. Patrick's, Sr. Alphonse's mother passed away, and not long after that, her father died. Sister Alphonse continued her weekly trips to the church, which she grew to love. When she reached adulthood, Sr. Alphonse converted to Catholicism and became a nun.

At first, Sr. Alphonse's older sister, who had become her primary caregiver, was furious with her! Eventually, the older girl relented. In fact, after viewing firsthand Sr. Alphonse's dedication, her sister also converted to Catholicism and took vows as a nun.

Bat Attack

I grew up in the shadows of St. Joseph Grammar School. The convent, across the lane from the school, bordered the street where we spent our days. There were no playgrounds or parks so we hung out in the street playing football and stickball amid passing cars. The nuns, aptly named Sisters of Charity, would come to the back convent door overlooking our street playground and recruit one of us to run errands. If caught, er, selected, it meant leaving whatever game was in progress. We weren't eager volunteers.

Despite the risk of being nabbed, we continued playing in the street. To offset the element of surprise from nuns sneaking up on us, we designated one boy to serve as our sentry. His job was keeping an eye on the convent's back door. At the slightest movement from one of the sisters, he yelled, "bat attack." Soon, we kids called him Bat Man and relied greatly on his patrol.

We were scruffy young boys in need of all the love we could get. Those wonderful women passed on their love and attention each time one of them stepped out the back door. Most of us didn't fully appreciate their goodness but, despite being young toughs, we still respected the sisters. Eventually, our esteem for them grew into love. I still recall their names, all those women who left their homes across the United States to shepherd our group of street sheep. God bless them all.

Offering Up Prayers

The nuns often offered up short prayers for others in need and taught us to do the same whenever we saw an ambulance or heard emergency sirens. In 1990 my husband and I were at the mall going our separate ways to run errands. I was headed toward a store when I saw in the distance an ambulance crew carrying out someone on a gurney. Just as the nuns taught me, I thought to myself, "I should pray for that man." I said a silent prayer on his behalf. When I got closer to him, I realized the man was my husband. He had suffered a major stroke. I didn't lose him that day; I was blessed to have him another nine years.

Sisters in Poetry

By the time we were in high school things were a bit different. Some of the nuns were very hard on us. Many years later, I was coming back to the United States after a trip to Ireland. On the plane were two nuns who had taught me; they were blood sisters as well. Both were from County Clare and headed to Alabama where they were stationed. We reminisced about times at St. Mary's in Limerick and I told them one of the things I attributed to the sisters was my great love of poetry.

Even though it may have seemed there were days they weren't getting through to us, they did, I reassured the sisters. I can still recite the poems they taught us. The sisters gave us many wonderful teachings and experiences, even though it might have taken a long time for us to realize it.

Lost Time

Sister Elizabeth told us, "Use your minutes, don't waste time. Spend five minutes to mend a sock, pick up something off the floor, clean the drawers." I've always remembered that and try to keep busy.

Do I Know You?

I attended Catechism classes after Sunday Mass every week until I enrolled in the Catholic high school. One year, my cousin, Sr. Mawn-awena, was our teacher. Boy, she was strict! In fact, my classmates teased me about her after class. Oddly enough, she never spoke to me on a personal basis. She never acknowledged we were related. This bothered me for many years.

Thirty years later I ran into her at my mother's funeral. She apologized for not acknowledging me or speaking to me while I was her student. Sister explained her mother superior forbade her to talk to me. Sadly, when Sister's own younger brother was in her class, she was not allowed to talk to him.

I think of all the years we wasted under that rule when we could have been friends.

Sister Secret

While serving in the military, I had orders to ship out to Vietnam under a top-secret security level. No one was to know I was there.

After arriving in 'Nam, I was instructed to fill out a Last Will and Testament. I also was to name two people I believed who could keep my whereabouts secret. These people would then be my go-between in case I was killed. Family and close friends were not permissible. Our leaders suggested naming former teachers or ministers.

The priest I named died shortly after my arrival in Southeast Asia, so the responsibility rested solely on the shoulders of a nun. Sister Columba kept the secret, and luckily for both of us, I returned safe and sound. Years later I was home on a visit and stopped by to see her at the convent. Sister showed me a stack of letters she had mailed to me in Vietnam telling me she didn't want to be the liaison. The letters had been sent back to her, edited by the military. She had no other way to reach me with her refusal. Thus, she kept the secret.

Big Ears

Some kid called me "big ears," so I got into a fistfight with him. Sister Helen broke up the fight and asked me how it started.

"He said I had big ears," I told Sister, pointing to the other boy.

Pulling me by my ears, Sr. Helen shouted, in front of the entire class,

"Well, you *do* have big ears, Michael. You are what you are. Stop fighting!"

I was devastated and humiliated by Sister's tirade. I now believe there may have been a method to her apparent madness. She had given me a lesson about accepting myself for who I was.

Late for Everything

I'm late for everything today and I trace it all back to my sophomore year at St. Mary's. Each morning, the routine was the same. Mom packed bologna sandwiches for my sister and me, Dad doled out dimes for milk, and we all piled into the station wagon for our daily haul to school. And we were always late.

My homeroom teacher, Sr. Francis, tired of my late arrivals, tried humiliating me into forgoing my tardy ways.

"Oh, *she's* late again," Sister said, trying to shame me in front of my classmates.

"I'm sorry, but it's my sister who makes us late."

"There you go again, blaming your sister," she said, getting in her final shot.

Another one of my teachers who wasn't a nun and knew of my circumstances suggested I tell Sr. Francis to knock it off. As if I would say that to a nun! I couldn't do it, but he could and did. I still remember the stunned look on her face—usually when I'm running late.

That's Rubbish!

The nuns taught us that it was our duty as students of St. Pious to keep the playground clean and neat. Before we were allowed back into the classroom after lunch recess, we were required to clear the area of all gum wrappers, scraps of paper, and other bits of trash. I worked diligently to pick up as much rubbish as I could. To this day, I'm almost neurotic about cleanliness and picking up clutter. I'm very good at cleaning!

Dedication

In my senior year, I took a second year of Spanish with a sister having a known heart condition. One day during class, I found Sr. Agatha in a horrible state. Her face was deep pink, bordering on purple. She had difficulty breathing and was crouched over in severe chest pain. My mother was a nurse, so I knew the signs of a heart attack. I asked Sr. Agatha if she would like an escort to the school nurse. She refused and attempted to continue teaching.

What I saw in class was unbearable. No other classmate seemed disturbed by her condition. I knew the worst was imminent. I was frightened for Sister Agatha's life. I lied, excusing myself to the bathroom, and ran to the school nurse's office. I described Sister's physical state in a worried manner. The nurse's eyes widened. She knew my mother was a nurse and that I understood more about health conditions than most teenagers.

The nurse advised me to return to class and she would be there soon. The next five minutes seemed like an hour. The nurse arrived and convinced Sr. Agatha that she needed medical care. As they walked out the door together, the nurse nodded at me and gave me a knowing, reassuring glance.

The next day, the nurse pulled me aside and said, "No matter what Sr. Agatha tells you, or what anyone else says, you did the right thing. Thank you so much." Sister Agatha was out for about three weeks. During that time, I often asked the nurse or principal about her recovery.

When she returned, I told her I was happy to see her back. She acted annoyed, scolding me with "You shouldn't have."

"Yes, I should have and I'd do it again," I replied, my eyes welling with tears. Sister Agatha looked at me through tears in her eyes. We both bowed our heads.

We never discussed the matter again. None of the other students appeared to have any reactions. No one else in the school ever mentioned it to me. I hadn't told my parents. There was a quiet reaction from teachers and staff, however. They treated me differently; I gained their respect.

If there was something I dreaded (and still do), it was attention focused upon me. Bullies throughout high school taunted me. As an obese teenager, I was in the lowest stratum of school society. I learned insignificance was the key to safety. The less attention I received, especially from teachers, the safer I was. At the end of the school year, the underclassmen threw us graduates a good-bye party. They voted for superlatives such as Biggest Flirt, Mr. Personality. They slapped me with Teacher's Pet. They made my life hell throughout school, continually tormenting me. It was one more act of abuse. The teachers, especially Sr. Agatha, were always kind. Sister Agatha was a gentle soul.

Despite the treatment the underclassmen gave me, I remain grateful I was able to help Sister Agatha. She lived to teach many other Spanish classes. I'm appreciative of her lessons, too, as I have relied on Spanish throughout my life.

Sister Agatha's dedication to her faith, teaching, her students, and Spanish was profound. Because of her enduring and selfless nature, Sr. Agatha was willing to continue teaching while suffering a painful heart attack. The memory of her dedication and sacrifice in that moment will always remain with me. I am humbled that she considered giving up her life on behalf of my fellow students and me.

She shouldn't have, but she did. For that, I am eternally grateful.

Sipping cocktails with one of the nuns who taught us was a bit surreal. Not because she was wearing a blue suit instead of a habit, or because she nursed an Irish coffee until the blarney shone in her cheeks, but because we were three adults reminiscing. We weren't teacher and students (even though both of us sat more than a hand-swat away from Sister), we were adults sharing forty-year-old memories. Her recollections weren't *exactly* the same as ours. While she recalled the eagerness our fourth-grade class showed in visiting the library, we remembered our enthusiasm was over a *National Geographic* issue shelved in the library featuring topless tribal women. Neither one of us could remember the article, but the experience of seeing our first pictures of naked ladies remains embedded in our brains.

Even more significant were her recollections of life as a nun teaching us. There wasn't much time during the school day to question Sister about her childhood or her homeland. Who knew Sister had brothers and sisters? We left school each afternoon without much thought to what the nuns did in their after-hours. Never would we have thought they enjoyed swimming, much less visited parishioners with pools in their back yards. Summer vacation for us meant three months not thinking of the sisters. We didn't realize they spent their time earning higher degrees or traveling far away assisting impoverished parishes.

We ended our visit with Sister with more than a nostalgic feeling; we walked away with a better understanding of the nuns who taught us. Too bad it took so many years.

M. P. and D. S.

Chapter Ten

"ISTER BARBARA, YOU PETRIFIED ME with your story about a little girl who died shortly after making her First Holy Communion," the woman told her former second-grade teacher, an elderly nun.

"I did? I don't recall that story."

"You said a girl prayed to die after she received her First Communion so that she could live with Jesus in heaven. Sure enough, before Mass ended, she was found dead in the pew. Still kneeling."

"'Wasn't it a good thing, too, for she certainly was in heaven,' you said. I prayed that God would take me like the little girl and then I secretly hoped He wouldn't. I kept going back and forth, 'God, take me please,' 'Please, God, I don't want to die.'

"I was terribly frightened."

Sister Barbara's faced turned ashen.

"That's *not* what I said. I talked about a little girl *already dying* who feared she wouldn't live long enough to make her First Communion. On her deathbed, an angel appeared to her and gave her communion. She died not long afterward, and yes, she most certainly would have been in heaven."

"Oops. I didn't exactly get the story right, did I, Sister?"

Nearly everyone who crossed paths with a nun—or those who had crossed a nun—has an "I remember Sister" story. In the spirit of the Brothers Grimm, Catholic storytellers have been regaling audiences with tales that began "Once upon a time, I had this nun..." which may or may not have ended happily ever after. Armchair historians popped out of their pews and dedicated themselves to preserving and passing along their Catholic heritage. They blathered on with tales dripping in nostalgia, recalling sisterly moments of amusement, admiration, respect, and even fear.

Most tales are decades-old recollections and sideline observations drawn from childhood experiences. As Sr. Barbara's anecdote demonstrates, memories blur and facts slip away over time. Former students, parents, and casual observers often paint lopsided pictures, thinking they're turning out a masterpiece when they're actually producing a *Whistler's Mother* with an empty rocking chair. Unless tellers have donned a veil and walked a mile in Sister's shoes, history fades with each retelling and life stories become nothing more than photocopies of photocopies. Whom can future generations trust for the real skinny?

Sister, of course.

Sisters have plenty of tales to share, starting with becoming a nun. Sitting in a classroom, it was easy for students to believe Sister Mary Joseph had no past but was plopped in front of them in full habit and already a hundred years old. The truth is, nuns were once young girls, running, laughing, and playing, when they got the call to join religious life.

Generally, there was no drama in a girl's calling to the sisterhood, no visions from St. Gertrude the Great, patron saints of nuns. Little girls didn't hover over the phone waiting to answer the winning *Dialing For Dogma* question: Do you want to dress in black from head to toe, change your name, and spend the rest of your life facing throngs of unruly kids? The invitation to join usually came as a silent tap on the shoulder or a quiet beckoning voice within their hearts and minds. Sometimes, examples of others were motivation enough.

"I thought about becoming a nun ever since I was nine years old when I met sisters back home in Ireland from assignment in Africa," said Sr. Catherine, a nun for more than fifty years. "When I joined their order several years later, I wanted to go abroad, preferably to a leper colony." Sister Catherine's father objected, so she did the next best thing. She volunteered for assignment in America.

"I had mixed feelings. I was excited about going to America but nervous and lonely at the thought of leaving my family and the sisters with whom I lived," she said.

Girls as young as thirteen hitched up with orders like the Franciscan Sisters of the Sacred Heart, Little Sisters of the Poor, and the Sisters of Charity. They committed to a multiyear process, beginning as postulants for one year and continuing for several years as novices. The girls had enlisted in God's army and were headed for basic training that would include years of study and preparation before they professed their final vows.

Just like recruits in the armed services, nuns-to-be were given a once-over by top brass before acceptance into the order. Like their military counterparts, superiors tried to weed out those not suited for religious life. They tried screening them during intake, or the postulant stage, where both recruits and leaders came together to see if there was a fit. Deferments might have been granted to those who couldn't hold muster. A conscientious objector might have been ignored but a case of flat feet probably could have sent a postulant walking. After all, it took strong arches to walk in a nun's shoes. During the postulant stage sisters-in-training learned the ropes and grew accustomed to daily routines.

A postulant's intake often began with a grueling interview where Mother Superior questioned her suitability for religious life. "Are you willing to get up each day at 4 A.M.?" "You won't be bored praying the rosary twice a day?" "You won't miss your family?"

After sticking out the getting-to-know-you phase, God's recruits packed their gear and headed off to boot camp. They were received into their orders as "novices," privates marching in the infantry. Sisterly G.I. Joes received haircuts, new uniforms, and the promise of energy-sapping drills.

At a religious ceremony resembling a wedding, postulants paraded into the chapel wearing traditional wedding gowns and veils while families and friends watched from pews. Receiving the clothing of their order and a new name, postulants left the church only to return wearing full habits, ready to officially become brides of Christ.

"We filed back into the church and each of us received her name. We didn't know what name would be chosen, even though we had submitted three requests each," said Rose, a former novice. "That was my first big lesson as a novice. I no longer had any control over my life, including choosing my own name."

God's young brides weren't ushered off to a Poconos honeymoon. They headed back to the motherhouse to pursue several more years of rigorous training and education. A key lesson was learning exactly how to walk the walk of sisterhood. In some orders, sisters were taught to stand erect, in a serene and dignified manner. Heads forward, eyes downcast, and no frowns, superiors ordered.

Girls were taught to develop a sense of community by working and praying together, yet creating intimate relationships with other sisters and lay people were discouraged. Having a close and personal relationship with Mother Superior was encouraged, though, and once a week, required. Each week, girls met for the "Chapter of Faults" where they reported sins they had committed. Mother Superior assigned penances and the girls prayed to correct themselves. Cutting rosary time by skipping a decade or two would guarantee face time with Mother Superior, as would merely *thinking about* skimping on the ritual. Girls were required to confess actions *and* thoughts. Not even Uncle Sam expected his recruits to let them know what was on their minds, which is wise. Mother Superior might hold up well to a confessor's "I wished you would jump off the bell tower" while Major General might have problems restraining himself.

Finally, novices professed final vows and sealed their lifetime re-enlistment with pledges of obedience, chastity, and poverty. Of all the promises, obedience proved the toughest. To "help" novices learn the art of obeying, some superiors used bell-ringing to develop conditioned responses among their charges. Bells rang and novices jumped quicker than Pavlov's dog could drool. They learned to stop whatever it was they were doing and take the expected action, such as gathering in the chapel.

"'No Bell' days were quite a luxury. Those days we had some flexibility, like getting up an hour later or saying prayers on our own time," Rose recalled.

Adjusting to their habits was nearly as tough for sisters as following orders. Some girls, being girls albeit sisters, grew enamored with their new look. A few, along with their families, saw the habit as a step up in society, a mark of prestige. It became a visible sign of their special calling. Divine intervention helped novices overcome such temptations of the cloth. Each morning before dressing, novices prayed over their habits. If that didn't work, mother superiors offered guidance.

"I was both awed and thrilled when I first put on my habit as a newly professed nun. I remember Mother's words to us, though: 'The habit doesn't make the nun,' said Sr. Catherine.

"I've always tried to keep that in perspective."

After final vows came deployment to the battlefield—their assignments. Some, like Sr. Catherine, shipped out to missions in faraway lands while many bustled off to parish schools in nearby communities. Either way, many were placed in classrooms. Oftentimes, their marching orders to teach came with little or no training.

"I was sent to instruct a class of forty-five students for six weeks, replacing a lay teacher who had quit," said Rosemary, a former nun. "The kids were wild, jumping out of the windows and running up and down the street.

"This came several years after my having had no contact with anyone other than my parents, and with no education training," she recalled. "For six weeks, I didn't smile or even crack a grin. I didn't dare.

"I guess it worked. The children behaved."

Settling in to classroom routine and getting over the fact they faced forty, fifty, and even sixty children, many sisters grew to enjoy their assignments. The "little enemy" had a way of tugging at their hearts. Children were curious lots, asking questions about God, heaven, and what was under a nun's habit.

"A little boy stared at me for a few minutes and asked, 'Sister, do you have ears?'" Sr. Catherine recalled from her days as an elementary-school teacher. "'Well, of course, I do.'"

"'Are you *sure*?'"

Children were intrigued by us, Sister explained, and honest, too. One child asked Sr. Catherine if she would teach her in heaven. More importantly, would Sister be teaching phonics in heaven? A little girl shared her worries with the nun from Ireland: "How can I become a sister if I'm not Irish?"

When not in the classroom or church, most sisters could be found in the convent, where they followed the same daily grind as other women of the day: cooking and cleaning. And since there were no men, sisters shared all household duties, including maintenance and repairs. Jobs were divvied up by individual qualifications. Women who knew the difference between a jigsaw and jigsaw puzzle took on handyman chores, while those who could crack walnuts under kneelers were bound for kitchen duty. Just because a sister stood over a hot stove didn't guarantee she knew what to do next.

"I was teamed up with Sr. Martha for dinner duty and rice was on the menu," Rosemary recalled. "There were nine of us, so Sr. Martha cooked one cup per person. She dumped nine cups of uncooked rice into the pot.

"We had rice all over the kitchen!"

Convent life wasn't driven entirely by rules and routines. Sisters threw in a little recreation, too. Some might have found relaxation in a nightly needlepoint project stitching *The Last Supper* or in the basement organizing a relic collection. Others enjoyed physical activities such as roller skating and swimming. Many shared a keen interest in sports, with baseball an overwhelmingly popular choice.

Still, a couple of nuns in Texas savored outdoorsman sports, even if it only took them a few feet out the convent's back doors. When asked how she and another young nun spent their spare time, Sr. Mary Jane said, "Shooting blackbirds resting on headstones in the cemetery" behind her convent. The nun was a West Texas native who grew up hunting with her dad and was as comfortable with a shotgun in her hand as she was with a crucifix.

Generation after generation of nuns adhered to strict standards, rituals, and dress codes and relied on their superiors for all decisions. Then came Vatican II, allowing a return to birth names, modernization of habits, and relaxation of rules. For many sisters, it allowed them to better fulfill vocations.

"Vatican II gave us greater freedom to serve the people and follow our calling without being hindered by outmoded rules," Sr. Catherine said.

Being good soldiers, sisters carried on. Some ventured out of the classroom and into the inner city. Health care, social work, and even prison ministry drew nuns out of their convents. A number of them left their orders altogether. In the forty years since Vatican II, many sisters have died. Some of those remaining live in retirement communities while others have ventured back to their homelands.

"Just as I was when I left Ireland, I am anxious about returning," Sr. Catherine said as she readied for her journey back to the home she left more than a half century earlier.

"I am nervous about leaving America, my home for most of my life, but it's time to go."

SISTERS' OWN MEMORIES

Sister Speaks: Answering a Call

Dowry

The day of my reception into my order as a novice was the first time I had seen my father in a year. I stood on a porch between the convent and chapel, wearing my bride's dress. My mother had sewn it herself.

"Dad, they expect you to give me $2,000 for a dowry," I said to my father. This was an unbelievable amount of money for my dad, a schoolteacher. I felt terrible for him. I didn't know how he would raise the money. Those worries were what I remembered most about that day.

Family Ties
Our order was very open-minded about relationships with our families. We were allowed to visit them after we made our final vows. I couldn't stay at my mother's house, though. I boarded in a local convent. We could go home every summer for a few days. My cousin, in the Ursuline order, wasn't allowed to visit her dying mother in the hospital, even though the hospital was in the same town as her order. She wasn't cloistered, either. She was allowed to visit a student in the hospital but not her own mother.

Permission Granted
The nun in charge of us postulants was known as our "Mistress." Basically, we had to earn her permission to do virtually everything. That included asking her if I could throw away my very, very patched and worn old ladies' underwear.

Divine Intervention
After one quick piano lesson, Mother decided I was proficient enough to play the church organ for a novena. I was a horrible pianist. I couldn't play a simple tune, much less songs for a novena. It was so upsetting to me that I did the only thing I could do—pray for a miracle. The next morning when I went to the church to play, I discovered that the organ was broken. I wouldn't be playing that day. My miracle was delivered.

Keeping Your Eyes to Yourself
I think often about "custody of eyes." That meant when walking down a corridor we were required to look straight ahead and not into the doorways we passed. I was a curious sort, so I at least had this to profess at weekly confession, along with being late for my charge or

chores. It was difficult to "sin" in a convent, other than breaking these rules of our order, and weekly confession was mandatory.

Tight Habit

After receiving the habit, it took me several weeks to be able to chew my food without pain. The coif surrounding my face was tight, and muscles I never knew I had were making themselves known to me!

Sister Speaks: A Day in My Life

Hot Habits

Our assignment was in South Florida during the '50s and '60s, when neither the school nor the convent was air-conditioned. We received special permission to wear white habits instead of our order's traditional black. Wearing them in the heat was horrible. Luckily we had so many changes. Most of Saturday was spent washing, starching, and ironing our habits.

Fluted Caps

Our Mother Provincial (Superior) was something of a "queen of the congregation" who ruled over us all. We were at a Mass celebrating a special anniversary for the school. The priest thanked all of us sisters for our hard work but didn't address Mother Provincial specifically. That threw her in a tizzy, and her fury headed in my direction.

Our habits included a circular, fluted cap with a veil. When we ventured in public, we were to pull the veil up over the caps as a sign of modesty. During Mass, Mother noticed some of the girls didn't have their veils flipped over their caps. She decided to check us all out, including me.

"Young Sister, you, up in the choir. Did you have your cap covered?" she asked me afterward in the convent.

"No, I don't believe I did, Mother." Mother Provincial gave me a dressing down like I'd not had before. I believe she was still angry over not being formally recognized at Mass.

Habit Memories

Our habits were made of heavy serge wool and they were awful to wash! We wore a large, heart-shaped plastic yoke around our neck over the cape of serge that covered our cotton shirtwaist. The top part sewn to the bottom serge was cotton so we were able to wash and hang it out frequently.

The habit was designed in the 1800s under the directive to wear clothing that was the dress of the day so that we could better blend in with the French community where our order began. Our founder didn't want us to be different. How ironic for those of us wearing the habit a hundred years later in steamy southern Louisiana. I think if the founder had been around he would have made some revisions.

Streetcar to Perdition

Mother Provincial (Superior) ordained that Sr. Lucy and I begin piano lessons each Saturday. The fact that neither of us possessed one iota of musical talent as proven by our spending years in piano lessons during grammar school where we grasped little more than the basics didn't figure into Mother's plans. We were doomed.

Those days, we taught (usually on the basis of a dead nun's teaching certificate) weekdays and attended education classes at Loyola on Saturdays from first thing in the morning until noon. Sister Lucy and I rode a bus and transferred to a streetcar to reach the university. Our return streetcar took as by a young piano instructor's apartment. Perfect, Mother Provincial thought. Dreadful, thought we.

Our instructor was talented, no doubt, and strictly business. Years later, when I became aware of such things, I surmised he was gay. Mother Provincial had ordained; she would never relent. I was overcome by the hopelessness. I was desperate to escape, but how?

One Saturday, our instructor gave us our out. In an effort to relax our hands, which were stiff from nervousness, he placed the top of his hands under our wrists and lifted them, encouraging us to "relax, relax." Our plans were born.

Mother Provincial appeared sufficiently horrified and forbade us to return when we gave her our concerned report:

"Mother, we thought you should know...he's playing with our hands."

Last Supper
We could not talk at a meal on a day that also was a professed sister's (saint's) feast day, so the meal was her choice. It was the first time I had ever eaten oyster soup—ugh! I couldn't even ask what it was and was obliged to clean my bowl. I have never eaten it since, and it has been forty years.

Mangled Mess
Laundry days called for us feeding an endless number of sheets into the massive mangle, which ironed all items flat, which we then folded. With our order's postulancy, novitiate, junior nuns (vowed on a yearly basis), professed nuns, infirmary and visiting nuns, we had plenty of sheets to launder. Those days were hot and long.

Sister Speaks: Living My Vocation

Tough Issues
One of the toughest issues I faced as principal during the late '60s in the South was the intolerance among my students. Some white children were very prejudiced against black people, saying they were "lazy" and "no good." I taught them laziness was not color-blind and was found in all races. Most importantly, God created us as equals. Each person, no matter his or her color, is a child of God and of infinite worth and dignity. It was a difficult lesson to get them to learn, considering the nature of the times.

Enough for a Band, or Two
Sister Eleanor's kindergarten classroom was right across the hall from me. She taught *ninety-nine* students! Sister was absolutely amazing. She even had them perform in a rhythm band at the end of the year. They were quite good. The funny thing was, she was an only child!

Having to manage so many little ones was such a challenge but she never complained.

Jailbirds

There were no methods-in-education classes, no supervised practice teaching experiences, and no special education credits in my background preparation to teach. No, but I was armed with my Provincial Superior's "obedience assignment" as the will of God that guaranteed my capabilities to teach all fourth-grade subjects to a class of forty-five students. Those children were at my mercy and I at theirs.

What I remember most from that first teaching assignment were Freddy and Sam. Freddy was a muscular, heavy, inattentive twelve-year-old and Sam was his wiry, fidgety chaos-creating thirteen-year-old brother. Both seemed to share the same goal in life: escaping the classroom learning experience. As a twenty-year-old in my first year of teaching, I wasn't prepared to deal with learning disabilities, so I concentrated on maintaining a safe environment for the rest of the students, especially when the two brothers attacked one another with open scissors flying across the classroom.

One October morning, confession day, I was organizing my class to march double-file across the playground to the church for their turn to confess their sins. Freddy and Sam, with uncharacteristic thoughtfulness, stayed behind to close the classroom doors.

Later that afternoon, I opened my desk drawer to find all fifteen tuition envelopes collected earlier in the day missing.

"Did anyone see a stranger come into my classroom at recess or noon?" I quizzed the children.

"No, Sister."

I reported the robbery to the principal, who immediately instructed me to search the students' bags. I tried deterring her with the assurance, "None of my children would do something like that. I sent the children home."

"She's young; she'll learn," the kindly Franciscan pastor answered.

As I later recalled, Freddy and Sam had gone to confession with the rest of the children. They were home free! I had forgotten about their burst of helpfulness.

The boys didn't return to class after the Christmas holidays. They had been arrested, caught with a master key to all the apartments in one of the projects after clues from repeated burglaries had led police to them. One of the detectives questioning the boys said Freddy and Sam possessed the clever minds of hardened criminals. They were jailed.

Did I question where I might have failed them? Not for one minute! Not even a "spouse of Jesus" could work that miracle.

Tabloid Tales

One of the first priorities of the newly assigned Methodist minister was a tour of our hospital and in particular, the obstetric department. His wife accompanied him; her near-term condition dictated their interest in our facility.

"We have been blessed with three girls, Sister," Reverend Gerth informed me, "all healthy and beautiful." Did I detect a wistful tone to his voice, a hopeful expression on his face?

Mrs. Gerth arrived in labor three weeks later, amid an explosion of other admissions to our obstetrics department. My shift had ended but I remained on duty to help the night crew.

As I circulated between the delivery room and the expectant fathers' waiting area announcing new arrivals to dads, I noticed Reverend Gerth sitting quietly, waiting. Then it was his turn.

Too hurried to absorb the significance of my announcement, I smilingly told him, "Reverend Gerth, you have a healthy, eight-pound baby boy."

He smiled, and blushing, started to rise out of his seat, and then hesitated. Instead, he murmured, "Thank you, Sister."

Not until later that day did Reverend Gerth explain his hesitancy upon hearing my good news for him. "When you told me we had a boy—a *boy*—my first instinct was to hug you! Luckily, I resisted. I had visions of tomorrow's newspaper headlines: METHODIST MINISTER HUGS CATHOLIC NUN."

Alas, a simple embrace might have made headlines forty years ago but today would create nary a second look.

Snack Thief

It was time for the children to pull out their midmorning snacks when I noticed Lorraine in distress.

"Sister, my snack is gone," Lorraine said "Someone took it." I had a pretty good idea who our snack thief might be. This wasn't the first time.

Hubert, sitting right behind Lorraine, had his hands buried in his pockets and looked nowhere but down at his desk. Hubert wasn't a bad boy, I just think he got hungry. I didn't dare ask him if he took the snack because he would only lie. I couldn't cause him to commit another sin, could I?

Instead, I instructed the children to take out pencils and papers. They were to write letters to God. In their letters, they were to thank God for their wonderful morning treat.

"Offer up a prayer for Lorraine, too, as her treat was taken by someone else," I said. Lorraine was a mature child, so I continued my talk. "Now, isn't it a shame that poor Lorraine will go hungry, even though her mother packed her a wonderful snack."

By this time, Lorraine had turned misty-eyed. So had Hubert.

"Here's what you do. If you stole the snack, please tell God in your letter and ask forgiveness. I won't read your letters," I said. "If you didn't steal it, just offer up your thanks."

The children put pencil to paper and the room was quiet as they jotted down their words. Hubert raised his hand.

"Yes, Hubert, what is it?"

"Sister, how do you spell 'stole'?"

I knew for sure the class thief's identity. That was the last of the stolen snacks that year.

Father Hayes

I had been teaching the children about the Sacrament of Baptism, in particular that when life-threatening emergencies arose, someone other than a priest could baptize a baby in danger. Teddy Hayes raised his hand.

"Sister, I baptized my baby brother," Teddy offered.

"Oh, have you, now? Tell us all about it," I asked Teddy, our class storyteller.

"My mother asked me to watch the baby for a few minutes while she took her bath. He started crying and wouldn't stop. I thought *I* was going to die so I held him under the faucet and baptized him."

I thought I would be the one to die! His classmates were impressed, however. From that day forward they called him "Father Hayes."

Monkey Business

Paul turned in his homework, dirty and tattered. He needed reminding to take more care.

"Paul, please try to be neater. Your homework is messy."

"Yes, Sister. Julia got a hold of it."

"Well, be more careful."

The next morning, I looked at Paul's homework, again a sloppy mess.

"Paul, this is horrible! What happened?"

"Julia got it again, Sister."

"Well, take more care."

Again, the next day Paul's homework was ripped and dirty. I had had it! "Paul, why is your homework such a mess? This is inexcusable."

"Sister, Julia keeps tearing it up!"

"Paul, please speak to your mother. Tell her to keep your little sister away from your homework." As soon as I said that, his classmates snickered.

"What in the world is so funny?"

"Sister, Julia isn't my sister. She's my pet monkey." At this, the class roared. It seems everyone but me knew Julia was a monkey. I made him bring it to school and show me. Yes, Julia was a monkey.

Civil Rights

Several of us sisters drove to Alabama one summer to visit a convent in Birmingham. It was during a time of upheaval; the Civil Rights movement was in full force. There was rioting in the streets, especially in the South.

When we reached the city, we took a wrong turn and got lost. Suddenly, we were driving down a street and dozens of black youths swarmed our car. They surrounded the car and rocked it back and forth. We were terrified.

Just as suddenly as the young men appeared, they backed off and created a gauntlet for us to pass through. As we drove away, I saw the boy responsible for securing our safe departure. He stood before us and blessed himself with the sign of the cross.

I believe some other sister must have treated that boy with kindness and taught him to do the same.

Glossary

Angelus—Series of prayers performed three times a day: morning, noon, and evening. Presumably, parents handled praying the Angelus with their children during morning and evening sessions but Sister took charge at noon. She had children on their knees for twenty minutes right before lunch. Children sometimes toppled over in hunger, which sisters often mistook for passionate devotion.

Baltimore Catechism—The book containing beliefs and teachings of the Catholic Church in a question-and-answer format. Created in 1884, it became the most popular religious text through the 1960s. Lessons called for Sister drilling students with questions such as "Who made you?" She expected rote answers in return. At one point, translations may have been under consideration, such as the Hoboken Catechism with "Who made youse guys?" and an Atlanta Catechism with "Who made y'all?"

Benediction—A short ceremony where the consecrated host (Jesus' body) is displayed for adoration. It was a favorite diversion to Sister's science experiments.

CCE—Uncertainty surrounds the actual definition of the abbreviation, but all agree it stands for the religious education given to Catholic Publics—students not enrolled in Catholic school. Some parishes call it Continuing Catholic Education while others refer to it as Catholic Christian Education. It followed generations-old CCD—first standing for Confraternity of Christian Doctrine and then transforming into Catholic Christian Doctrine. A new title, Faith Formation, has been popping up in parishes. Regardless of the name, CCE was first taught by sisters and, later, by moms. Children in Catholic school weren't taught CCE or CCD. They were taught religion.

Chapter of Faults—Sessions within religious communities where participants come before superiors to admit their faults and infractions against the rules of their orders. Many sisters brought the process into the classroom. A steady glare at a student could bring a child to his knees, confessing more transgressions than he would in the confessional. Children preferred Chapter of Faults over the Book of Faults, fearing the latter might be thrown at them.

Cloister—A monastic community where the religious live in seclusion is considered "cloistered." Despite coincidences of living as a hermit and exhibiting quirky behavior, Howard Hughes was not a member of a cloistered community.

Coif—A close-fitting cap and cowl worn under nuns' veils that covered chins and necks. Many suspect it was designed by a mother superior trying to hide her double chin and turkey neck.

Confession—The sacrament of reporting sins to the priest and receiving forgiveness from God. To acclimate students to the ritual, sisters often practiced with children and pretended to be the priest. Some nuns' theatrics were convincing. Youngsters forgot they were pretending and alerted Sister to classroom shenanigans.

Confessional—An enclosed room the size of a small closet where the priest hears confessions. Although the room was scary, it did provide the security of anonymity. The out-of-the-way box turned into an ideal secret hideaway for errant children.

Confirmation—The sacrament where Catholic children receive the gift of the Holy Spirit in order to make them strong Christians. Sisters emphasized children were becoming soldiers in Christ's army. The sacrament called for students renaming themselves after a saint they admired. Kids saw it as the chance to become known as Isabel instead of Harriet or Rufus instead of Christopher. Very few chose saints' names popular among nuns for fear of being labeled Sister's pet.

Confiteor—A general profession of sins usually prayed at the beginning of Mass and said during special occasions. Classroom recitation after Sister discovered a rotten banana shoved in her desk drawer was not a Church-sanctioned occasion.

Consecration—The most solemn part of the Mass when the priest changes the bread and wine into the body and blood of Christ. As sacrilegious as it sounds, this was the only moment when a child could successfully shoot a spitwad. Sister's head remained bowed in reverence for a full thirty seconds.

Crucifix—A cross bearing the likeness of Jesus crucified, and another favorite trinket sisters gave to children. Crucifixes were awarded to the crème de la crème—students who spent recess cleaning out messy kids' desks.

Dogma—Teachings of the Catholic Church revealed by God. All members of the Church must fully accept them—just like Sister's words.

Ejaculations—Bursts of short prayers such as "Jesus, Mary, and Joseph" and usually accompanied by the sign of the cross. For some reason, the term no longer exists in Catholic lexicon.

First Holy Communion—The sacrament when Catholics first receive Jesus' body in the form of a consecrated host. Boys and girls dressed entirely in white, which proved challenging. Staying away from dirt mounds on the way to the church gave boys fits while more than one girl tripped because she couldn't see the steps through her veil.

Genuflection—Kneeling on one knee when entering a Catholic church as a way of honoring Christ's presence. It also was a gesture used by brown-nosers entering the classroom and sucking up to Sister when they had forgotten their homework.

Holy Cards—Wallet-size cards with an illustration of a saint on one side and a prayer or devotion on the other. Sisters awarded cards to students for good behavior, improved grades, or just because they had cleaned out her desk. Children tried trading them with the Publics for gum and treats but all they got for them were black Good & Plenty candies and sticks of clove gum.

Holy Water—Ordinary water blessed by a priest and used by Catholics as they entered and left a church. Despite rumors, the water was not made holy by having the hell boiled out of it.

Holy Water Fonts—Containers holding holy water and placed in entryways to churches, classrooms, and homes. Sisters gave students plastic holy water fonts so the children could hang them in their bedroom doorways.Without sisters hovering over them, children neglected blessing themselves while at home, and fonts mildewed.

Infallibility—The freedom of error in teaching Church matters of the faith. Only the pope's word can be infallible, although most students believed a nun's word had to be.

I.N.R.I.—Abbreviation found on the crucifix meaning "Jesus of Nazareth, King of the Jews." Children spent hours trying to figure out why the initials didn't match the words.

Legion of Decency—An organization created in 1934 to fight immoral movies. Catholics stood up in church and publicly pledged to not attend morally objectionable movies as well as theaters that showed morally objectionable films. This pledge went out the window by the time *Two Mules For Sister Sara* hit the big screen. Not even the legion could convince Catholics to say no to Clint Eastwood.

Lent—The forty days before Easter when sisters encouraged children to "give up" treats like chocolate or episodes of *My Favorite Martian*. Most children complied but secretly preferred giving up nightly homework.

Limbo—The place where babies go if they die before being baptized. Baptisms were scheduled for the Sunday after a baby came home from the hospital "just in case." Currently, the concept of limbo is in limbo.

May Crowning—An annual procession and ceremony honoring Mary early in May. A lucky girl—usually the one Sister relied on to dust convent furniture—earned the honor of placing a crown of fresh flowers on a statue of Mary. Sometimes sisters lined up alternate crowners, sort of like runners-up in beauty pageants, to step in at the last moment if the chosen girl was unable to fulfill her duties.

Mea Culpa—Latin expression meaning "through my fault." It was a quick prayer, accompanied by chest-thumping and head-bowing. Nuns liked charging kids caught sticking bubble gum under the pew with this prayer because they didn't bring their rulers into church.

Novena—A nine-day devotion or prayer to obtain special graces. Newspaper classified-ad salesmen are partial to the Novena to St. Jude because the prayer must be published once the nine days are completed.

Nunmobile—Nickname for the convent car, usually a station wagon. Sisters never traveled alone; six or seven piling in and out of the nunmobile resembled a circus clown act.

Pagan—Heathen; one who has little or no religion. Before Vatican II, some sisters taught that "pagans" included anyone not Catholic. Since then, the definition covers some Catholics, as well.

Penance—During the sacrament of Confession, the actual prayers assigned by the priest for absolution of sins. Sisters would have made great priests with the creative penances they dished out.

Publics—Both Catholic and non-Catholic students who attended public school. Envious of Publics for not having to pray the Angelus every noon, and for not having to wear ties and beanies to school, children in Catholic school blamed Publics attending Saturday CCD for everything that went missing in the classroom.

Purgatory—A "holding cell" where people go after they die but before they enter heaven. It's now viewed as a state of purification, a process of becoming clean or pure enough to enter heaven. This soul-washing station sounds much less frightening than descriptions some sisters shared: a place just as hot as hell, you just didn't stay there for eternity. (Sisters serving in the deep south during the '50s and '60s probably thought they had been assigned to purgatory.)

Relics—Remains of a dead saint, usually a piece of their clothing, hair, or bones. Relics are kept as a memorial to a departed saint. Sisters saw them as prized giveaways. While Publics received bookmarks from their teachers, Catholic-school kids were awarded with old bones.

Rosary—A revered devotion to Mary that reflects upon Jesus' life, praying the rosary relies on repetition of the Hail Mary and other prayers in fifteen sets of ten, along with the use of beads to keep track. It was very often recited after lunch, causing some children to nod off.

Sacrament—An outward, visible sign of God's grace. Knowing the importance of these signs, Sisters devoted an extraordinary amount of time teaching and practicing them. While non-Catholic second graders spent afternoons playing tag, Catholic children practiced kneeling and sucking, not chewing, pieces of bread.

Sanctus—Latin for "saint" and uttered just before the consecration during Mass. "Cut it out" sometimes followed when an altar boy rang the bells too long during the consecration.

Scapular—Originally an outer part of a garment draped over the shoulders like the yokes worn by monks and some orders of nuns, the scapular evolved into a necklace with two pieces of cloth the size of postage stamps strung together by what appeared to be a shoelace. Sisters taught children to never take them off and to wear them tucked inside blouses and shirts. Many old women boasted wearing the same scapular without removing it for thirty years but dirty, grimy Catholic kids kept scapular salesmen in business by getting replacements every couple of years.

Sin (venial, mortal)—The act of purposely turning away from God; long considered a transgression against God's will. Mortal sins were the most egregious and kept sinners out of heaven. Venial, or lesser, sins didn't keep a sinner from heaven but the more one had, the longer his or her stay in purgatory. For children taught by nuns, virtually anything they thought, said, or did constituted a sin. How much they ticked off Sister determined whether the sin was venial or mortal.

Sodality of Mary—An organization of women and girls dedicated to the devotion of Mary and the practice of community service. Projects might have included babysitting parishioners' children during Sunday Mass and serving meals at the Senior Saints luncheon each month. Each time a baby puked on a Sodality Girl, or an elderly woman pinched her cheek, sisters were convinced the girl moved closer to entering the convent.

Stations of the Cross—Also known as the Way of The Cross, stations are a set of pictures or statues symbolizing Jesus' last steps on earth. Many times during the year, especially in Lent, sisters escorted children in a procession through the stations. The ritual, calling for a reflection of Christ's sufferings and death at each station, included genuflecting at each of the fourteen stops. As well as helping a young child feel Christ's pain, performing the Stations of the Cross marked a Catholic's first steps toward knee-replacement surgery later in life.

Tabernacle—A cupboard on the altar housing consecrated hosts. Tabernacles are locked and have been built to withstand floods, storms, and curious hands. The units traditionally were constructed from metal, making dusting for fingerprints easy.

Transubstantiation—The act of changing bread and wine into Christ's body and blood by a priest during Mass. Sisters used the term sparingly, as some of the boys sometimes confused it with "masturbation."

Vatican II—The Second Vatican Ecumenical Council opened in 1962 and closed in 1965. Its purpose was to create a spiritual renewal of the Church and become "Aggiornamento"—Pope John XXIII's word describing that the Church needed to be brought up to date and adapt itself to modern times. Not in his wildest dreams did he think it would call for radical changes like allowing nuns to expose their legs.

Contributors

Adams, Betsy
Chapter 6: "Crowing Like a Rooster"
Anton, Arthur D.
Chapter 9: "The Sister Slap"
St. Patrick Elementary; Sacred Heart High School
Sedalia, MO
Archer, Anna
Chapter 4: "Hair Clips"
Dalhart, TX
Arnold, Patrick M.
Chapter 6: "Who's the Babe in the Woods?"
Camden Catholic High School; 1958–1964
Barlow, Cory (McAllister)
Chapter 7: "Could You Repeat That, Sister?"
St. Sylvester's School, Brooklyn, NY; 1960–1968
St. Michael High School, Brooklyn, NY; 1968–1972
Barthelemy, Jerry
Chapter 5: "Sister Sleds"
Chapter 5: "Holy Rollers"
Chapter 5: "Stuffed Love"
Chapter 6: "Ruler Fee"
Chapter 6: "Sincerely Yours"

Charlton, Sue
Chapter 4: "Exposing Hem"
Maria Regina High School, Seaford, NY; 1966–1970
Cowles, Delia C.
Chapter 9: "Sisters in Poetry"
St. Mary's, Limerick, Ireland; twelve years
Cramer, Kathy
Chapter 2: "Bloody Hankie"
Chapter 4: "Duck's Ass"
Chapter 4: "You Want to Look Up...Oh, a Number?"
Marian Catholic, Chicago Heights, IL; 1960–1964
Crann, Ed
Chapter 6: "Group Slap"
Chapter 6: "Sister Bulldog"
Our Lady of the Lake, Verona, NJ; 1956–1965
Our Lady of the Valley High School, Verona, NJ; 1965–1969
Currie-Wood, Margie (Freeman)
Chapter 3: "Just Hanging Around"
St. Mary Magdalene, San Antonio, TX; 1956–1963
Deran, Paul
Chapter 5: "Nosing Around"
Chapter 6: "Is It Sr. Jeckyll or Sr. Hyde?"
Chapter 7: "Knockout"
Chapter 7: "Music to Her Ears"
Saint James, Falls Church, VA; 1961–1966
Devlin, James Patrick
Chapter 3: "Whirling Dervish"
St. Ambrose Catholic, Houston, TX
St. Pius X High School, Houston, TX
Donohoe, Brenda (Arnold)
Chapter 3: "Invisible Ink"
St. Luke Catholic School, Lake Worth, FL
Dorey, Corinne
Chapter 2: "Grandma and the Nuns Know Best"
St. Luke Catholic School, Lake Worth, FL; 1964–1972

Durant, Richard
Chapter 3: "World's Finest Chocolate or Latin"
St. Joseph High School, North Adams, MA
Ecsedy, Stephen R.
Chapter 6: "No More Yardsticks"
St. Rosalia, Pittsburgh, PA; 1945–1953
Central Catholic, Pittsburgh, PA; 1953–1957
Eichelberger, Brenda
Chapter 4: "Bye-Bye, Birdie"
St. Phillip The Apostle, Camp Springs, MD
Fazzino, Kim
Chapter 2: "Basketball Trash"
Furbeck, Irene (Ashton)
Chapter 3: "Boxing Match"
St. Matthew, Edison, NJ; 1965–1973
St. Pius X High School, Piscataway, NJ: 1973–1977
Gallagher, Richard
Chapter 3: "Hey John, Is That You?"
Bishop Kenrick, Norristown, PA
Gerardi, Mary (Behrens)
Chapter 2: "Paper in Trash"
Holy Cross Elementary, Champaign, IL; 1950s
Graham, Elizabeth
Chapter 2: "Limbo Babies"
Chapter 5: "Hey, Good Lookin'"
St. Agatha's Primary School, Kingston-upon-Thames, UK; 1969–1975
St. Catherine's Senior School, Twickenham, UK; 1975–1982
Habel, Mary Lou (Wilson)
Chapter 2: "Protestant Kneeling"
Chapter 4: "Safety-Pin Snafu"
Chapter 7: "Walkout"
St. Cecilia and St. Hubert Catholic High School for Girls, Philadelphia,
PA
Haig, Catherine
Chapter 4: "Seeing Red"
Bishop McDonnell Memorial High School, Brooklyn, NY; 1948–1952

Hawkins, Maggie (Frederick)
Chapter 9: "Pointer Theory"
St. Bonaventure and Our Lady of Mt. St. Carmel, Toronto, Ontario, Canada

Hebda, Karen
Chapter 7: "Rubber-Band Girl"
St. Ambrose, Grosse Pte Park, MI; 1958–1970

Herbert, Edward
Chapter 2: "Are You Kneeling?"
St. Brigid, Ridgewood, NY; 1960–1969

Hewitt, Diane (Fioravanti)
Chapter 6: "Spanking Machine"
St. Jerome School, East Rochester, NY; 1957–1965
St. Agnes High School, East Rochester, NY; 1965–1966

Hogwood, Gayle
Chapter 8: "Sister Dottie"

Johnson, Karen (Alsback)
Chapter 4: "World War II"
Chapter 5: "Pink Nightgowns"
Chapter 9: "Driving Nuns"
Chapter 9: "Late for Everything"
Mater Dei High School, New Monmouth, NJ; 1971–1975

Kennedy, Joan
Chapter 7: "Loose Chicks"
St. Patrick Elementary and High Schools, Elizabeth, NJ; 1950–1956

Kertz, Marie Herbert
Chapter 2: "J. M. J."
Chapter 9: "There Go I"
Chapter 9: "Offering Up Prayers"
New Orleans, LA; eight years

Kraft, Margie (Di Carlo)
Chapter 6: "Spitting Boy"
Chapter 7: "Cup Runneth Over"
Holy Saviour School, Norristown, PA; 1961–1969
Bishop Kenrick, Norristown, PA; 1969–1973

Laferriere, Richard
Chapter 4: "Cruising the Streets"

Michaels, Karen
    Chapter 2: "I'll Chew if I Want To"
    Chapter 4: "Shoulder Tap"
    Chapter 5: "Naked Nuns"
    Villa Cabrini Academy, Burbank, CA: 1951–1960

Mytych, Louis P.
    Chaper 6: "Where's Your Homework?"
    St. Joseph, Yonkers, NY; 1961–1968
    Sacred Heart High School, Yonkers, NY; 1969–1972

Olivo, Lynn
    Chapter 5: "Miss Purple"
    Holy Spirit High School, Atlantic City, NJ; 1959–1963

Osborne, Richard
    Chapter 9: "Sr. Irma's Pitch"
    St. Jerome School, Cleveland, OH; 1956–1962
    Holy Cross School, Euclid, OH; 1963–1965
    St. Joseph High School, Cleveland, OH; 1965–1969

Pierpont, Chuck
    Chapter 5: "Medieval to Modern"
    St. Mark, Baltimore, MD; 1966–1969
    St. William of York, Baltimore, MD; 1969–1976

Quaresima-Patrick, Rose
    Chapter 10: "Permission Granted"
    Chapter 10: "Keeping Your Eyes to Yourself"
    Chapter 10: "Last Supper"
    Chapter 10: "Tight Habit"
    Chapter 10: "Mangled Mess"
    St. Mary's Grade School, Plainfield, IL; four years
    St. Francis Preparatory/Academy, Joliet, IL; four years as aspirant
    Sisters of St. Francis, Joliet, IL; one year postulant; three months novice: Sr. M. Monica Anne, O.S.F.
    College of St. Francis, Joliet, IL; four years during convent and afterward

Rooney, Sheila
    Chapter 3: "A National Treasure Falls"
    Chapter 3: "Trilingual Education"
    Chapter 4: "Sex Segregation"

Taylor, John Wm
Chapter 9: "Special Guidance"
Turk, Joseph (Joe)
Chapter 9: "Whispering Hope"
Saints Cyril & Methodius, Sheboygan, WI; four years
Valles, Tamara Jeanne
Chapter 1: "Sister Bon Bon Lives On"
St. Roch's School, Staten Island, NY; 1988–1991
Notre Dame Academy High School, Staten Island, NY; 1991–1995
VanVleet, Carmella
Chapter 5: "What Was That Odor?"
Walsh, Bill
Chapter 3: "Detroit Tigers"
Chapter 9: "Redhead Boy"
St. Hugo's, Detroit, MI
Webster, William
Chapter 3: "Latin Hummingbirds"
Chapter 6: "Faster Than a Whacking Ruler"
Chapter 7: "Baseball Trading Card"
Chapter 7: "Car or Nun Trouble"
Wehe, Peggy (Carter)
Chapter 6: "Shameful Demerits"
Chapter 5: "Want Fries with That?"
St. Patrick, San Diego, CA; 1950–1958
Rosary High School, San Diego, CA; 1958–1962
Worth, Claudia (Ruffert)
Chapter 3: "The Conductor"
Holy Family School, Denver, CO
Wysatta, Mike
Chapter 2: "Christ the King Procession"
Chapter 4: "Golden Boy"
Fort Worth, TX; 1958–1970
Zimmerman, Linda H.
Chapter 4: "Such a Tease!"
Bishop Gibbons High School, North Tonawanda, NY; 1962–1966

Sources / Bibliography

Chapter One
1. John J. Fialka, *Sisters: Catholic Nuns and the Making of America* (New York: St. Martin's Press, 2003), 172.
2. John J. Fialka, *Sisters: Catholic Nuns and the Making of America* (New York: St. Martin's Press, 2003), 200.
3. Ibid.

Chapter Two
1. *"Baltimore Catechism"* [online]. Available on the World Wide Web: http://www.catholic.net/teaching_the_faith/template_article.phtm/?channel_id=14&article.

Chapter Four
1. Socrates, *The Columbia World of Quotations, 1996* [online]. Available on the World Wide Web: http://www.bartleby.com.66/45/54545.html.

Chapter Five
1. Virginia Satir, *Wisdom Quotes* [online]. Available on the World Wide Web: http//www.wisdomquotes.com/0005555.html.
2. *Women's Intellectual Contributions to the Study of Mind and Society* [online]. Available on the World Wide Web: http://www.webster.edu/~woolflm/satir.html.

Chapter Six
1. "The Blues Brothers Movie Script" [online]. Available on the World Wide Web: http://corky.net/scripts/bluesbrothers.html.

Chapter Eight
1. Mary Higgins Clark, *Kitchen Privileges* (New York: Simon & Schuster, 2002), 39.

Chapter Nine
1. Michelle Perry, "Devito's *War of the Roses* a witty, wicked black comedy" [online]. *The Tech* 109, no. 56 (1989) 9. Available on the World Wide Web: http://www.tech.mit.edu/v1o9/n56/roses.56a. html.
2. Tim Russert, *Big Russ & Me: Father and Son: Lessons of Life* (New York: Miramax Books, 2004), 155.
3. Karen Trotter Elley, *First Person BookPage*, "Nora Roberts deals with destiny in Three Fates" [online]. Available on the World Wide Web: http://www.bookpage.com/0204bp/nora_roberts.html.
4. "A Talk with Oprah Winfrey" [online]. *BusinessWeek Online*. Available on the World Wide Web: http://businessweek.com/magazine/content/04_48/63910414.htm (November 29, 2004).

BIBLIOGRAPHY

Books

1. Ekstrom, Reynolds R. and Rosemary. *Concise Catholic Dictionary for Parents and Religion Teachers.* (Mystic, CT: Twenty-Third Publications, 1982).
2. Johnson, Kevin Orlin, Ph.D. *Why Do Catholics Do That?* (New York: Ballantine Books, 1994).
3. Klein, Rev. Peter. *The Catholic Source Book* (Orlando: Harcourt Religion Publishers, 2000).
4. O'Gorman, Bob and Faulkner, Mary. *The Complete Idiot's Guide to Understanding Catholicism* (Indianapolis: Alpha Books, 2000).
5. Rejnis, Ruth. *The Everything Saints Book* (Avon, MA: Adams Media Corporation, 2001).

Web Resources

1. "The Chapter of Faults" [online]. Available on the World Wide Web: http.societyoftheimmaculata.com/chapter.html.
2. "Nun" [online]. Available on the World Wide Web: http://mb-soft.com/believe/txh/nun.htm.
3. "Distinction between nun and religious sister" [online]. Available on the World Wide Web: http://wikipedia.org/wiki/NUN.
4. "From Postulancy to Profession" [online]. Available on the World Wide Web: http://www.olamshrine.com/olam/nun_progression.htm.
5. Mary Ann Strain, C.P. "Ask a Catholic: What vows does a nun take?" [online]. Available on the World Wide Web: www.cptryon.org/ask/vows.html.
6. "Thesaurus Precum Latinarum" [online]. Available on the World Wide Web: http://home.earthlink.net/~thesaurus.
7. "Catholic Online—Saints" [online]. Available on the World Wide Web: http://www.catholic.org/saints.
8. "Catholic Encyclopedia" [online]. Available on the World Wide Web: http://www.newadvent.org/cathen.
9. "New Catholic Dictionary" [online]. Available on the World Wide Web: http://www.catholic-forum.com/saints/indexncd.htm.

Video

1. *Brides of Christ*, Executive producers Penny Chapman and Liam Miller, 1991, The Australian Film Finance Corporation Pty Limited, Roadshow Coote & Carroll Pty Limited, Radio Telefis Eireann, Australian Broadcasting Corporation, 1991; A&E Networks, Hearst/ABC/NBC, 1994, videocassette, three videos, approximately 100 minutes ea.

Share Your Memorable
Nun Stories!

Send us your own nun story or memory for inclusion in an upcoming book, *WHAT WOULD SISTER DO?* Stories should be be less than 100 words but longer submissions may be considered. If you're not a writer but have a great tale, contact us for an interview. Acceptance of a story doesn't guarantee submission. Be sure to include a phone number, address, or active e-mail so you can be contacted.

E-mail:	nunstories@yahoo.com
Call or fax toll-free:	1.877.NUNBOOK
Mail:	Nunstories, P. O. Box 6555, Kingwood, TX 77339
Web:	www.nunstories.com

About the Authors

DANIELLE SCHAAF is a public relations consultant and lives in Houston with her husband and three children. She attended Catholic school in South Florida for eight years where, early on, nuns told Danielle she was a cheeky girl. She still is.

MICHAEL PRENDERGAST is an attorney and lives in Jacksonville, Fl. with his wife and two children. He attended Catholic school in South Florida for eight years where he drove the sisters nuts with his constant fidgeting. Thankfully, he's replaced that habit with text messaging from his cell phone.

DANIELLE AND MICHAEL are lifelong friends, beginning in first grade at Catholic school. Both have a caustic sense of humor, sloppy handwriting, and a penchant for following rules—all of which they attribute to their years with the nuns. As authors, they hope to honor the sisters who taught them by invoking vows of poverty. There's been no mention of vows of celibacy and obedience.